D1105493

GABY'S LATIN AMERICAN KITCHEN

BY GABY MELIAN

OTHER COOKBOOKS BY AMERICA'S TEST KITCHEN KIDS

The Complete Cookbook for Young Chefs
#1 *New York Times* best seller, 2019 IACP Cookbook Award winner for Children, Youth & Family

The Complete Baby and Toddler Cookbook
2020 IACP Cookbook Award nominee for Children, Youth & Family

The Complete Baking Book for Young Chefs
New York Times best seller, 2020 IACP Cookbook Award winner for Children, Youth & Family

My First Cookbook

The Complete DIY Cookbook for Young Chefs
2021 IACP Cookbook Award nominee for Children, Youth & Family

The Complete Cookbook for Young Scientists

The Complete Cookbook for Teen Chefs

PRAISE FOR AMERICA'S TEST KITCHEN KIDS

"The inviting, encouraging tone, which never talks down to the audience; emphasis on introducing and reinforcing basic skills; and approachable, simplified recipes make this a notable standout among cookbooks for kids." —*Booklist*, starred review, on *The Complete Cookbook for Young Chefs*

"A must-have book . . . a great holiday buy, too." —*School Library Journal*, on *The Complete Cookbook for Young Chefs*

"Inspiring not just a confidence in executing delicious recipes but encouraging [kids] to build foundational kitchen skills." —The Takeout, on *The Complete Cookbook for Young Chefs*

"What a great way to encourage a child to find fun in the kitchen!" —Tribune Content Agency, on *The Complete Cookbook for Young Chefs*

"The perfect gift . . . Any kid who spends enough time with this book will learn enough to at least make their own school lunches—if not the occasional family meal." —Epicurious, on *The Complete Cookbook for Young Chefs*

"For kids who are interested in cooking . . . [*The Complete Cookbook for Young Chefs*] introduces kids to all the basics . . . and of course there's a whole lot of easy and very tasty recipes to try." —NPR's *Morning Edition*, on *The Complete Cookbook for Young Chefs*

"Having cooked through several cookbooks from America's Test Kitchen, I have come to expect thoroughness, thoughtfulness, attention to detail and helpful troubleshooting, all of which create delicious results. It comes as no surprise that when ATK decided to create a cookbook for kids, *The Complete Cookbook for Young Chefs*, the same standards applied." —*Dallas Morning News*, on *The Complete Cookbook for Young Chefs*

"America's Test Kitchen has long been a reliable source of advice for home cooks. The kitchen tests tools, techniques and recipes before making recommendations through its TV show, magazines and cookbooks. Now, all that know-how is becoming accessible to kids in *The Complete Cookbook for Young Chefs*." —NPR, on *The Complete Cookbook for Young Chefs*

"This book makes baking accessible . . . An inclusive and welcoming text for young chefs." —*Booklist*, on *The Complete Baking Book for Young Chefs*

"A must-have book to keep your young adult cookbook section up-to-date and to support the current trend of creative young bakers. A contemporary and educational cookbook that's once again kid-tested and kid-approved." —*School Library Journal*, starred review, on *The Complete Baking Book for Young Chefs*

"The cooks at America's Test Kitchen have done a wonderful job of assembling appetizing and slyly audacious recipes for babies and young children." —*The Wall Street Journal*, on *The Complete Baby and Toddler Cookbook*

"This wonderfully interactive, non-messy introduction to baking, though especially designed for preschoolers, will be an instant hit with readers of all ages." —*School Library Journal*, on *Stir Crack Whisk Bake*

"The story is a fun concept, and Tarkela's realistic digital illustration offers the pleasing details of a television studio." —*Publishers Weekly*, on *Cookies for Santa*

"Many 11-year-olds like to get in the kitchen. With this cookbook, they can make over 70 delicious recipes. The best part, however, is that the cookbook explains why food cooks the way it does, and it includes science experiments they can do in the kitchen." —*Insider*, on *The Complete Cookbook for Young Scientists*

"A comprehensive cookbook designed for and tested by teen cooks . . . The layout is crisp and clear, starting with ingredients and their prep, with required equipment highlighted for easy visibility." —*Kirkus Reviews*, starred review, on *The Complete Cookbook for Teen Chefs*

"Kids will love the colorful site and its plentiful selection of recipes, projects, and cooking lessons." —*USA Today*, on the America's Test Kitchen Kids website

Copyright © 2022 by America's Test Kitchen

All rights reserved. No part of this book may be reproduced or transmitted in any manner whatsoever without written permission from the publisher, except in the case of brief quotations embodied in critical articles or reviews.

Library of Congress Cataloging-in-Publication Data is on file with the publisher.

AMERICA'S TEST KITCHEN

21 Drydock Avenue, Boston, MA 02210

Printed in Canada

9 8 7 6 5 4 3 2 1

Distributed by Penguin Random House Publisher Services

Tel: 800.733.3000

FRONT COVER

Photography: Armando Rafael

Illustrations: Gabi Homonoff

By: Gaby Melian

This book is dedicated to my abuela Porota, you are the reason why I cook!

America's Test Kitchen Kids

Editor in Chief: Molly Birnbaum

Executive Food Editor: Suzannah McFerran

Executive Editor: Kristin Sargianis

Deputy Food Editor: Afton Cyrus

Associate Editors: Tess Berger, Katy O'Hara, Andrea Rivera Wawrzyn

Photo Test Cook: Ashley Stoyanov

Assistant Test Cook: Kristen Bango

Editorial Assistant: Julia Arwine

Creative Director: John Torres

Art Director: Gabi Homonoff

Photography Director: Julie Bozzo Cote

Photographer: Kevin White

On-Location Photographer: Armando Rafael

Food Styling: Ashley Moore, Gina McCreadie, Chantal Lambeth, Catrine Kelty, Joy Howard, Shelia Jarnes, Kendra Smith

Photography Producer: Meredith Mulcahy

Photo Shoot Kitchen Team:

> Test Kitchen Director: Erin McMurrer
>
> Manager: Alli Berkey
>
> Lead Test Cook: Eric Haessler
>
> Test Cooks: Hannah Fenton, Jacqueline Gochenouer, Gina McCreadie, Christa West
>
> Assistant Test Cook: Hisham Hassan

Project Manager, Publishing Operations: Katie Kimmerer

Senior Print Production Specialist: Lauren Robbins

Production and Imaging Coordinator: Amanda Yong

Production and Imaging Specialists: Tricia Neumyer, Dennis Noble

Lead Copy Editor: Rachel Schowalter

Copy Editors: Katrina Munichiello, April Poole

Chief Creative Officer: Jack Bishop

CONTENIDO (CONTENTS)

DESAYUNO (BREAKFAST)

CHIPA (CHEESE BREAD)
26

BIZCOCHITOS DE GRASA (LITTLE FAT BISCUITS)
28

MANTECA (BUTTER)
32

MERMELADA DE FRUTILLA (STRAWBERRY JAM)
36

MANGÚ CON LOS TRES GOLPES (MASHED GREEN PLANTAINS WITH EGGS, CHEESE, AND SALAMI)
38

GALLO PINTO (RICE AND BEANS)
42

CHILAQUILES VERDES (TORTILLA CHIPS WITH GREEN SALSA, CHEESE, BEANS, AND FRIED EGGS)
44

BALEADAS (FLOUR TORTILLAS WITH BEANS, CHEESE, AND CHORIZO)
48

AREPAS CON QUESO (CORN CAKES WITH CHEESE)
50

HUEVOS PERICOS (SCRAMBLED EGGS WITH SCALLIONS AND TOMATOES)
54

PAN CON PALTA (BREAD WITH AVOCADO)
56

ALMUERZO (LUNCH)

LLAPINGACHOS (POTATO CAKES)
60

PUPUSAS (CORN CAKES WITH BEAN AND CHEESE FILLING)
62

CEVICHE DE CAMARÓN (SHRIMP CEVICHE)
66

SINCRONIZADA (HAM AND CHEESE QUESADILLA)
68

SÁNDWICH DE MILANESA DE POLLO (BREADED CHICKEN SANDWICH)
70

ARROZ CHAUFA (PERUVIAN FRIED RICE)
74

CACHAPAS (CORN PANCAKES)
76

BUÑUELOS DE ACELGA (SWISS CHARD FRITTERS)
78

COMPLETOS CHILENOS (CHILEAN HOT DOGS)
80

CHIVITO URUGUAYO (STEAK, HAM, CHEESE, AND FRIED EGG SANDWICH)
82

TACOS DE CARNE MOLIDA (GROUND BEEF TACOS)
84

MEDIALUNA OLÍMPICA (HAM, CHEESE, AND EGG CROISSANT)
86

HUEVOS DUROS (HARD-BOILED EGGS)
87

MERIENDAS Y BEBIDAS (SNACKS AND DRINKS)

EMPANADAS DE POLLO (CHICKEN TURNOVERS)
90

PICADA ARGENTINA (ARGENTINEAN-STYLE TAPAS)
94

SOPA PARAGUAYA (PARAGUAYAN "SOUP" CORNBREAD)
96

GUACAMOLE CON TOTOPOS (GUACAMOLE WITH TORTILLA CHIPS)
98

ELOTES (CHEESY CORN ON THE COB)
100

MIS NACHOS FAVORITOS (MY FAVORITE NACHOS)
102

TOSTADAS DE FRIJOLES Y QUESO (BEAN AND CHEESE TOSTADAS)
104

SÁNDWICH TOSTADO "CARLITOS" DE JAMÓN, QUESO, Y TOMATE (TOASTED HAM AND CHEESE SANDWICH WITH KETCHUP)
106

LA PIZZA RÁPIDA DE MI ABUELA (MY ABUELA'S QUICK PIZZA)
108

AGUA FRESCA DE LIMÓN (LIME WATER)
110

AGUA FRESCA DE FRESA (STRAWBERRY WATER)
112

AGUA FRESCA DE SANDÍA (WATERMELON WATER)
113

LICUADO DE BANANA (BANANA SMOOTHIE)
114

LICUADO TUTTI FRUTTI (ALL-THE-FRUITS SMOOTHIE)
116

CHOCOLATE CALIENTE (HOT CHOCOLATE)
118

CENA (DINNER)

ROPA VIEJA (SHREDDED BEEF STEW)
122

GUISO DE LENTEJAS (LENTIL STEW)
126

PASTEL DE PAPAS (BEEF SHEPHERD'S PIE)
128

PICADILLO (GROUND BEEF HASH)
130

ENTRAÑA AL HORNO CON CHIMICHURRI (OVEN-BAKED SKIRT STEAK WITH CHIMICHURRI SAUCE)
132

CAUSA DE ATÚN (COLD TUNA AND POTATO CASSEROLE)
134

ARROZ CON POLLO (RICE WITH CHICKEN)
138

MOQUECA DE CAMARÓN (SHRIMP STEW)
142

GAZPACHO (CHILLED TOMATO SOUP)
144

TOMATES RELLENOS (STUFFED TOMATOES)
146

ZAPALLITOS SALTEADOS (STIR-FRIED ZUCCHINI)
148

ZAPALLITOS REVUELTOS (STIR-FRIED ZUCCHINI WITH SCRAMBLED EGGS)
149

GUARNICIONES Y SALSAS (SIDES AND SAUCES)

FRIJOLES NEGROS (BLACK BEANS)
152

ARROZ BLANCO (WHITE RICE)
154

TOSTONES CON MOJO DE AJO (FRIED GREEN PLANTAINS WITH GARLIC DIPPING SAUCE)
156

MADUROS (FRIED SWEET PLANTAINS)
160

YUCA FRITA CON MAYONESA DE CILANTRO (FRIED YUCA WITH CILANTRO MAYONNAISE)
162

HUEVOS FRITOS (FRIED EGGS)
166

CURTIDO (CABBAGE SLAW)
168

CEBOLLAS EN VINAGRE (PICKLED ONIONS)
170

PICO DE GALLO (CHOPPED FRESH SALSA)
172

CHIMICHURRI (CHIMICHURRI SAUCE)
174

ENSALADA MIXTA (MIXED GREEN SALAD)
176

ÁRBOL DE NAVIDAD DE ENSALADA RUSA (RUSSIAN SALAD CHRISTMAS TREE)
178

POSTRE (DESSERT)

CHOCOTORTA (NO-BAKE CHOCOLATE COOKIE AND DULCE DE LECHE LAYER CAKE)
184

PASTEL DE TRES LECHES CON COCO (THREE MILKS CAKE WITH COCONUT)
186

ALFAJORES DE MAICENA (SANDWICH COOKIES WITH DULCE DE LECHE)
188

ARROZ CON LECHE (RICE PUDDING)
192

BRIGADEIROS (CHOCOLATE FUDGE BALLS)
194

ENSALADA DE FRUTAS (FRUIT SALAD)
196

PANQUEQUES CON DULCE DE LECHE (CREPES WITH DULCE DE LECHE)
200

SIGUE COCINANDO. SÉ FELIZ.
(KEEP COOKING. BE HAPPY.)

¡Hola! My name is Gaby Melian, and I am a professional chef. I have also been a teacher, a nanny, a street vendor selling empanadas, and a test kitchen manager.

I was born and raised in Buenos Aires, Argentina. There, I went to school to become a journalist. Later, when I came to the United States to visit my family, I loved it so much that I decided to stay.

I became a chef in New York City after I went to culinary school there, but really, I've always cooked. I grew up watching my abuela, my mom's mom, cook in our tiny kitchen in Buenos Aires. She started teaching me when I was very young. You'll find inspiration from my abuela throughout this book—from Mermelada de Frutilla (page 36) to La Pizza Rápida de Mi Abuela (page 108) to Pastel de Papas (page 128). She was a creative cook and a force in the kitchen who hated waste and loved to experiment. A lot of the dishes in this book from Argentina come directly from the kitchen we cooked in together when I was a little girl.

Today, I live in Jersey City, New Jersey, one of the most diverse cities in the world. I run Gaby's Kitchen, which is exactly that: my kitchen here in my apartment, where I cook and create videos, all with the help of my dog, Pucho. Cooking is what makes me truly happy, and I hope that it will make you happy, too!

¿POR QUÉ LATINOAMÉRICA?
(WHY LATIN AMERICA?)

I am Latina. I am from Argentina, a country in Latin America, which consists of México, plus many countries in South America, Central America, and the Caribbean. The countries that form Latin America are each so different and so culturally rich in their own ways. They have their own traditions, foods, and flavors— a combination of influences from Indigenous peoples and the colonizers who arrived from Europe. It would be impossible to cover all of Latin America in one cookbook, so this is from my perspective—the recipes I grew up eating and the recipes I've learned from my friends and neighbors.

Growing up, I didn't know people from all over Latin America. Just those from the neighbors of Argentina—Uruguay, Paraguay, Chile, Brasil, and Bolivia. But when I moved to New York City, I really learned about Latin America. After traveling 5,298 miles from my home in Argentina, I found myself in a city full of Latin American food and culture. Life works in funny ways, right? So this book is filled with recipes from my childhood in Argentina and those that I learned to love here in the United States.

Long before I became a chef, I learned to cook by watching and asking questions. This is the cookbook I wish I had growing up. I am writing it for my young self, and for you, to teach you about my past and the world outside your door.

PROBADO Y APROBADO POR NIÑOS
(KID TESTED AND KID APPROVED)

This cookbook is kid tested and kid approved. That means that there are thousands of other kids, just like you, out there who made these recipes, shared them with their friends and family, and loved the process and the results. When making this book, we had more than 15,000 kids test these recipes and send us feedback, letting us know what worked well and what could use improvement. You'll see a handful of these recipe testers in the pages of this book—both in photographs and in quotes. Thank you to everyone who helped make the recipes in this book as delicious as possible!

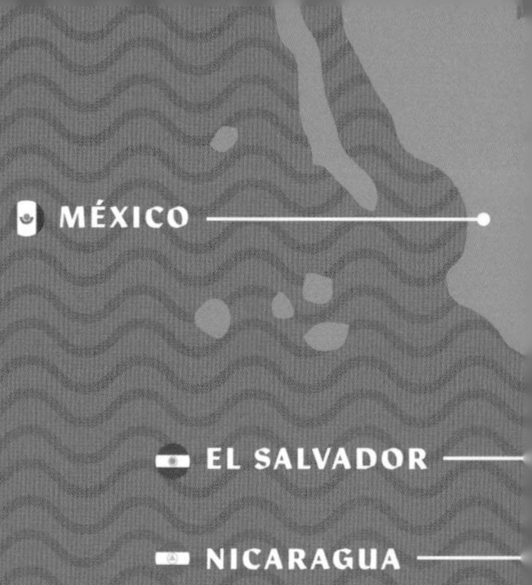

MÉXICO ——————

EL SALVADOR ——

NICARAGUA ——

¿DÓNDE ESTÁ LATINOAMÉRICA?
(WHERE IS LATIN AMERICA?)

Different people define Latin America in different ways, some based on geography, others based on history or languages spoken. On this map are what I think of as the countries and territories of Latin America. They include México, countries in South America, Central America, and some of the islands in the Caribbean Sea. You'll also see these countries and flags on the different recipes across this book. Which ones would you like to visit first?

CÓMO USAR ESTE LIBRO (HOW TO USE THIS BOOK)

There are a few things that are helpful to know as you start cooking from this book.

First, you'll be able to see which country each dish comes from via the flag and country name at the top of each recipe.

 Argentina

And to help you find the right recipe for you, I've rated each recipe with the skill level required.

 BEGINNER RECIPE

 INTERMEDIATE RECIPE

 ADVANCED RECIPE

A NOTE ABOUT SALT

I use **kosher salt** in every recipe in this book (except for a few, in which I call for flake sea salt). If you're using **table salt**, use **half** of the amount listed in the recipe, otherwise your dish will end up way too salty!

Finally, I like to be organized when I enter the kitchen to cook, so these recipes are written in a way to help you get organized, too!

¡EN SUS MARCAS! Ready!

After you read the recipe, start by preparing all your ingredients. This is also often called "mise en place"—a French term for "everything in its place." It guarantees that you won't forget anything or realize too late that you don't actually have any masarepa in your kitchen!

¡LISTOS! Set!

You're almost ready to start cooking . . . but not quite. You'll want to gather all the cooking equipment that you'll need before you start, too.

¡FUERA! Go!

Now it's go time. Start cooking, have fun, and be happy!

CONSEJOS PARA COCINAR (COOKING TIPS)

Here are a few things I ALWAYS like to keep in mind when I am cooking.

LÁVATE LAS MANOS (WASH YOUR HANDS)

This is perhaps one of the most important notes. It's important to wash your hands before you start cooking and every time you touch raw meat, seafood, or eggs. But, really, there is never a time when washing your hands once more will be wrong!

¡TODO ESTA CALIENTE! (EVERYTHING IS HOT!)

I cannot stress this one enough. Even as a professional chef with years of experience cooking in kitchens, I still need to remind myself of this one often. After turning off the heat, I like to put a dish towel or oven mitt over the handle of any hot pots or pans to help me remember that they're hot.

CHEQUEA DOS VECES (CHECK TWICE!)

When in doubt, always double-check! Read the whole recipe more than once before you start cooking to make sure that you understand what you're getting into.

VACÍA EL FREGADERO (EMPTY YOUR SINK)

This is a big rule I have when cooking at home. No matter what you're cooking, at some point in a recipe you're probably going to need to use the sink (to wash ingredients or drain potatoes, for example). So do not start cooking with a sink full of dishes! Trust me, you'll thank me later!

PREGÚNTALE A UN ADULTO (ASK A GROWN-UP)

When in doubt, never hesitate to ask a grown-up for help. This is written into many recipes where I know young chefs will want a bit of grown-up support. But if you're ever wondering if maybe you'd like some help, or if you're not sure about what you're doing, ask a grown-up!

UTENSILIOS DE COCINA
(KITCHEN EQUIPMENT)

Here is the kitchen equipment I use over and over again—and you will, too.

8-inch and 13-by-9-inch metal baking pans

Saucepans (large, medium, and small)

Chef's knife

Paring knife

Cutting board

Traditional skillet (12-inch)

Dutch oven (6 to 7 quarts)

KNIVES

COOKWARE & BAKEWARE

Nonstick skillets (12-inch and 10-inch)

Bowls (large, medium, and small)

Rimmed baking sheet

Oven mitts

KITCHEN BASICS

Cast-iron skillet

Parchment paper

Dish towel

Glass pie plate

Aluminum foil

Plastic wrap

Citrus reamer

Scale

Vegetable peeler

Food processor

Stand mixer

PREP TOOLS

Can opener

SMALL APPLIANCES

Blender

Measuring spoons

Ruler

Box grater

Electric hand mixer

Dry measuring cups

Liquid measuring cup

Flexible bench scraper

12-cup muffin tin

COOKING & BAKING TOOLS

Rasp grater

Icing (offset) spatula

Whisk

Ladle

Colander

Pastry brush

Tongs

Rolling pin

Spatula

Wooden spoon

Potato masher

Slotted spoon

Fine-mesh strainer

SPANISH GLOSSARY

ABUELA grandmother
AGRIDULCE sweet and sour
AGUACATE or **PALTA** avocado
AJO garlic
ALMUERZO lunch
AMASAR to knead
ARMAR to assemble
ARROZ rice

BEBIDAS drinks
BUDARE a clay or iron plate

CALIENTE hot
CARNE meat
CEBOLLA onion
CENA dinner
CHIVITO goat
COCINAR to cook
COL or **REPOLLO** cabbage
CORTAR to cut

DESAYUNO breakfast
DULCE sweet

FORMAR to shape
FREÍR to fry
FRESA or **FRUTILLA** strawberry
FRIJOLES beans

GRASA fat
GUARNICIONES sides

HORNEAR to bake
HUEVOS eggs

LICUADO smoothie

MANTECA or
MANTEQUILLA butter
MERIENDAS snacks
MEZCLAR to mix

PAÍS country
PAN bread
PAPAS potatoes
PELAR to peel
PICANTE spicy
PICAR to mince (like garlic)
POLLO chicken
POSTRE dessert

QUESO cheese

RALLAR to grate or shred
REPULGUE crimped edge
(like on an empanada)
RES beef

SALSA sauce
SALTEADO a stir-fry
SOBRAS leftovers

TEXTURA texture

**UTENSILIOS DE
COCINA** kitchen equipment

VACAS cows

MIS INGREDIENTES FAVORITOS (MY FAVORITE INGREDIENTS)

Here are some of the ingredients I use over and over in my kitchen!

DULCE DE LECHE I also call it heaven on earth. This "milk jam" is basically milk and sugar cooked together until it is thick, gooey, and delicious. Taste it for yourself in Alfajores de Maicena (page 188) and Chocotorta (page 184).

MASA HARINA Masa harina is a type of flour made by drying and grinding masa dough, which is made from corn that has been nixtamalized, or soaked in an alkaline solution to change both its flavor and structure. It's used to make tortillas, tamales, and Pupusas (page 62).

MASAREPA This type of flour is made by drying and then grinding precooked corn. It's used to make Arepas con Queso (page 50).

QUESO DE FREÍR Also called queso para freír, this fresh white cheese is very interesting because it does not melt when you cook it, it just softens. That makes it perfect for frying, as I do in Mangú con Los Tres Golpes (page 38).

QUESO FRESCO A firm, fresh cheese similar to feta. I like to eat it crumbled into Baleadas (page 48), or sprinkled onto Chilaquiles Verdes (page 44) and Tostadas de Frijoles y Queso (page 104).

SALAME DOMINICANO A large pre-cooked sausage made of pork and beef, used in Mangú con Los Tres Golpes (page 38). It's sometimes called salchichón dominicano.

CREMA This tangy sauce is a little thinner than sour cream and used on everything from Tacos de Carne Molida (page 84) to Tostadas de Frijoles y Queso (page 104).

TOTOPOS In México, tortilla chips are called totopos. They are toasted, fried, or baked triangles of corn tortillas. Find them in Guacamole con Totopos (page 98) and Mis Nachos Favoritos (page 102).

PLÁTANOS These relatives of bananas are firm and green when unripe and soft and black when ripe. They are often fried to make Tostones con Mojo de Ajo (page 156) or Maduros (page 160).

SAZÓN In Puerto Rico and parts of Central America, sazón is the name given to a popular spice blend. But it's also a Spanish word that means "seasoning," or the way each chef adds "flavor" to their dishes.

HOW TO MEASURE AND WEIGH

For consistent cooking results, it's important to measure accurately. There are two ways to measure ingredients: by weight, using a scale, or by volume, using measuring cups and spoons. Using a scale to weigh your ingredients is the most accurate method. But if you don't have a scale, that's OK! On this page are tips on using a scale and how best to measure ingredients if you don't have a scale.

HOW TO USE A SCALE

1. Turn on the scale and place a bowl on the scale. Then press the "tare" button to zero out the weight (that means that the weight of the bowl won't be included!).

2. Slowly add your ingredients to the bowl until you reach the desired weight. Here we are weighing 5 ounces of all-purpose flour (which is equal to 1 cup).

HOW TO MEASURE DRY AND LIQUID INGREDIENTS

Dry ingredients and liquid ingredients are measured differently. Note that small amounts of both dry and liquid ingredients are measured with measuring spoons.

Dry ingredients (flour, sugar, masarepa) should be measured in dry measuring cups—small metal or plastic cups with handles. Each set has cups of various sizes. Dip the measuring cup into the ingredient and sweep away the excess with the back of a butter knife.

Liquid ingredients (milk, water, juice) should be measured in a liquid measuring cup. Set the measuring cup level on the counter and bend down to read the bottom of the concave arc at the liquid's surface. This is known as the meniscus line.

HOW TO CHOP AND SLICE ONIONS

1. Halve the onion through the root end, and then use your fingers to remove the peel. Trim the top of the onion.

2. To chop: Place the onion halves flat side down. Starting 1 inch from the root end, make several vertical cuts.

3. Rotate the onion and slice across the first cuts. As you slice, the onion will fall apart into chopped pieces.

4. To slice: Place the onion halves flat side down. Trim off the root end and discard it. Then slice the onion vertically into thin strips (follow the grain—the long stripes on the onion).

HOW TO PEEL AND MINCE GARLIC

Garlic is sticky, so you may need to carefully wipe the pieces of garlic from the sides of the knife to get them back onto the cutting board, where you can cut them. You can also use a garlic press to both crush and mince garlic.

1. Crush the clove with the bottom of a measuring cup to loosen the papery skin. Use your fingers to remove and discard the papery skin.

2. Place 1 hand on the handle of a chef's knife and rest the fingers of your other hand on top of the blade. Use a rocking motion, pivoting the knife as you chop the garlic repeatedly to cut it into very small pieces.

HOW TO CHOP FRESH HERBS

Fresh herbs need to be washed and dried before they are chopped.

1. Use your fingers to remove the leaves from the stems; discard the stems.

2. Gather the leaves into a small pile. Place 1 hand on the handle of a chef's knife and rest the fingers of your other hand on top of the blade. Use a rocking motion, pivoting the knife as you chop.

HOW TO ZEST AND JUICE CITRUS

The flavorful colored skin from lemons, limes, and oranges (called the zest) is often removed and used in recipes. If you need zest, it's best to zest before juicing. After juicing, use a small spoon to remove any seeds from the bowl of juice—or work over a fine-mesh strainer.

1. To zest: Rub the fruit against a rasp grater to remove the colored zest. Turn the fruit as you go to avoid the bitter white layer underneath the zest.

2. To juice: Cut the fruit in half through the equator (not through the ends).

3. Working over a bowl, push the pointed end of a citrus reamer into the cut side of the fruit and twist to release the juice.

HOW TO SLICE AND CHOP BELL PEPPERS

1. Use a chef's knife to slice off the top and bottom of the bell pepper. Remove the seeds and stem.

2. Slice down through the side of the pepper. Press the pepper so that it lies flat on the cutting board.

3. Slice the pepper crosswise (the short way) into thin strips. (To chop the pepper, turn and slice the strips crosswise into small pieces.)

HOW TO STEM, SEED, AND MINCE CHILES

Chiles contain a compound called capsaicin that makes them spicy. To make sure that you do not get it on your skin or in your eyes, wear disposable gloves when touching chiles.

1. To stem: Hold the chile firmly with 1 hand, with the stem facing out. Use a chef's knife to slice off the stem and top of the chile.

2. To seed: Cut the chile in half lengthwise (the long way). Use the tip of a teaspoon to scoop out the seeds and ribs from each half. Discard the seeds, ribs, and stem.

3. To mince: Press 1 half of the chile so that it lies flat on the cutting board, skin side down. Slice the chile lengthwise (the long way) into ¼-inch-wide strips. Repeat with the remaining chile half.

4. Turn the strips and cut crosswise (the short way) into ¼-inch pieces. Repeat with the remaining chile half.

HOW TO GRATE OR SHRED CHEESE

When grating or shredding, use a big piece of cheese so that your hand stays safely away from the sharp holes.

1. To grate: Hard cheeses such as Parmesan can be rubbed against a rasp grater or the small holes of a box grater to make a fluffy pile of cheese.

2. To shred: Semisoft cheeses such as cheddar or mozzarella can be rubbed against the large holes of a box grater to make long pieces of cheese.

HOW TO SIFT

Place a fine-mesh strainer over a large bowl. Add the flour or cocoa powder to the strainer and tap the side of the strainer to sift the flour or cocoa powder into the bowl.

Desayuno
Breakfast

CHIPA
(CHEESE BREAD)

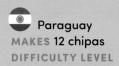 Paraguay

MAKES **12 chipas**

DIFFICULTY LEVEL

¡EN SUS MARCAS! Ready!

●●•●•●●●●●●••●●●

INGREDIENTS

1 tablespoon **olive oil**

2 cups (8 ounces) **tapioca flour**, plus extra for the counter

2 tablespoons **unsalted butter**, cut into ½-inch pieces and softened

2¼ cups shredded **gouda cheese** (9 ounces) (see page 21)

1 **large egg**

⅓ cup (2⅔ ounces) **milk**

1 teaspoon **kosher salt**

¡LISTOS! Set!

●●●●●●●●●●●●●●●●●●

EQUIPMENT

12-cup muffin tin

Large bowl

Flexible bench scraper or wooden spoon

Ruler

Oven mitts

Cooling rack

The first time I tried chipa, a bread from Paraguay made of cheese and tapioca flour, I immediately fell in love. It was the late 1980s—so about 40 years ago now!—and I was traveling with my mom and some friends. My friend Ofe was from Paraguay, so he brought us to all his favorite hidden places to eat. We were in the capital city, Asunción, which is one of the oldest cities in South America and right next to my home country of Argentina. He brought us to Mercado 4, a crowded market full of colorful fruits and vegetables, sounds, and smells—and all kinds of street vendors. Ladies carried baskets of warm chipa on their heads, selling the freshly baked bread in sizes big and small. I tried one. A big one. I shared it with my friends. It was warm and chewy and tasted like butter and cheese. Now at home in New Jersey, I like to make my chipa into small buns so that I don't need to share. Once you taste one you'll go back for more!

1. Adjust an oven rack to the middle position and heat the oven to 400 degrees. Use your fingers to grease the inside bottoms and sides of a 12-cup muffin tin well with the olive oil. Wash your hands.

2. Add the tapioca flour and softened butter to a large bowl. Use your hands to work the butter into the flour until it is incorporated and the mixture looks like coarse sand—it will still look really dry.

3. Add the gouda and mix with your hands until all the cheese is coated with flour. Make a well in the center of the flour mixture and add the egg, milk, and salt. Mix with a flexible bench scraper until the dough starts to come together. Use your hands to mix the dough until it is well combined and starts to form a ball.

4. Lightly sprinkle extra tapioca flour over a clean counter. Transfer the dough to the floured counter, then knead, portion, and shape the dough following the photos below.

5. Place the muffin tin in the oven. Bake until the chipas look puffed and lightly golden brown with darker cheesy spots, 15 to 18 minutes.

6. Use oven mitts to transfer the muffin tin to a cooling rack (ask a grown-up for help). Let the chipas cool for 10 minutes. Gently wiggle the chipas to loosen them from the muffin tin and transfer them directly to the cooling rack. Serve warm—chipas taste best when they are freshly baked!

CÓMO AMASAR Y FORMAR LA MASA (HOW TO KNEAD AND SHAPE THE DOUGH)

1. Transfer the dough to the lightly floured counter and knead it until the dough comes together, 1 to 2 minutes (the dough will still be slightly crumbly—this is OK!). If the dough is still a bit dry, wet your hands and continue kneading.

2. Use your hands to roll the dough into a 12-inch log, about 1½ inches thick. Use the bench scraper to cut the dough into 12 equal pieces (about 2 ounces each).

3. Gently roll each piece of dough into a ball, cupping your hands (the same way you make meatballs!). If the dough gets sticky, put a little bit of extra tapioca flour on your hands. Place each ball into the greased muffin tin.

BIZCOCHITOS DE GRASA

(LITTLE FAT BISCUITS)

Bizcochitos de grasa, which literally translates as "little fat biscuits," are a simple breakfast and snack staple in Argentina. And they are what they sound like: small biscuits made traditionally with tallow (though I like to use lard or butter). They are generally served plain alongside a mug of yerba mate tea. Sometimes I like to finish mine with a sprinkle of sugar (see page 30). And I'm no stranger to spreading my bizcochitos with a little homemade butter (page 32) and strawberry jam (page 36). For the kneading steps of this recipe, I recommend having a little bowl of flour nearby—you will need extra flour at some point, and you do not want to dig in the flour container with your wet hands!

Argentina
MAKES **30 bizcochitos**
DIFFICULTY LEVEL

INGREDIENTS

- 3½ cups (17½ ounces) **all-purpose flour**, plus extra for the counter
- 1 tablespoon **kosher salt**
- 2¼ teaspoons **instant** or **rapid-rise yeast**
- 1 teaspoon **sugar**
- 8 ounces **lard** or 16 tablespoons **unsalted butter**, cut into ½-inch pieces and softened
- 1 cup (8 ounces) room-temperature **water**

¡LISTOS! **Set!**

EQUIPMENT

Large bowl

Flexible bench scraper or wooden spoon

Dish towel

Rimmed baking sheet

Parchment paper

Rolling pin

Ruler

2-inch round cutter

Fork

Oven mitts

Cooling rack

¡FUERA! **Go!**

1. Add the flour, salt, yeast, and sugar to a large bowl and mix well with your hands. Add the softened lard to the flour mixture and work it with your hands until there aren't any visible pieces of lard.

2. Make a well in the center of the flour mixture and add the room-temperature water. Use a flexible bench scraper to start mixing the flour and water together until a dough starts to form. When the dough is formed (see photo 1, page 31), cover the bowl with a dish towel and let it rest for 10 minutes on the counter.

3. Adjust an oven rack to the middle position and heat the oven to 375 degrees. Line a rimmed baking sheet with parchment paper.

KEEP GOING

4. Lightly sprinkle extra flour over a clean counter. Transfer the dough to the floured counter. Knead, roll, and cut the dough into bizcochitos, following photos 2–4 on the far right.

5. Gently prick each bizcochito a couple times with a fork. Let them rest for 10 minutes.

6. Place the baking sheet in the oven. Bake until the bizcochitos rise and turn a pale golden brown, 15 to 18 minutes.

7. Use oven mitts to transfer the baking sheet to a cooling rack (ask a grown-up for help). Let the bizcochitos cool for 10 to 15 minutes. Serve. (The bizcochitos can be stored in an airtight container for up to 3 days—though I don't know anyone who has had any last for that long!)

BIZCOCHITOS AGRIDULCES (SAVORY-SWEET BIZCOCHITOS)

I like to make "bizcochitos agridulces," which are a savory-sweet version of the traditional bizcochitos. After you've placed your bizcochitos on the parchment-lined baking sheet in step 4, use the tip of your finger to rub a tiny bit of **water** on top of each bizcochito and then sprinkle on a little bit of **sugar**. You can also try a bit of **salt** (or salt AND sugar), **herbs**, or anything else that comes to mind. Don't be afraid to experiment.

" IT WAS FUN TO ROLL AND CUT OUT THE BISCUITS. IT WAS FUN TO MIX THE DOUGH WITH MY HANDS. THEY TASTED GOOD, AND MY DAD ATE A BUNCH OF THEM AS SOON AS HE COULD."

—Evie, age 9

1. Use a flexible bench scraper to start mixing the flour and water together until a dough starts to form. When the dough is formed, cover the bowl with a dish towel and let it rest for 10 minutes.

2. Sprinkle the counter lightly with extra flour. Transfer the dough to the counter and knead it with your hands until it's smooth, about 5 minutes—your arms might start to hurt, but trust me, the end results are worth it!

3. Rub a little bit of flour on a rolling pin. Use the rolling pin to gently flatten and roll the dough into a 12-inch circle, about ¼ inch thick.

4. Dip a 2-inch round cutter in extra flour and use it to cut the bizcochitos, cutting them as close together as you can. Place the bizcochitos on the parchment–lined baking sheet, leaving about ¼ inch between each bizcochito. Gather the leftover scraps of dough and gently knead them back together. Let the dough rest under a dish towel for 10 minutes. Roll the dough out to ¼-inch thickness and cut more bizcochitos. You should have about 30 bizcochitos total.

MANTECA
(BUTTER)

I grew up eating pan con manteca y mermelada (bread with butter and jam) washed down with a big cup of café con leche (coffee with milk). Yes, I drank coffee as a kid! I grew up in a house filled with family—my mom, aunts, cousins, and my abuela. My abuela did a lot of cooking, as you'll read about throughout this book, but I actually learned about making butter at school, from my fourth grade home economics teacher. This isn't just a recipe—it's a magical activity being able to watch cream turn into butter. Good, tasty butter comes from good, tasty cream. I prefer to use organic heavy cream for this recipe. If you like your butter salty, the next time you spread some of your homemade butter on toast or crackers, sprinkle a little bit of flaky salt on top. On my pan con manteca, I love a little bit of sea salt plus a drizzle of honey or a spoonful of homemade jam (page 36).

 Argentina

MAKES 1 cup

DIFFICULTY LEVEL

¡EN SUS MARCAS! Ready!

INGREDIENTS

- 4 cups **water**
- 3 cups **ice cubes**
- 2 cups **heavy cream**

¡LISTOS! Set!

EQUIPMENT

Fine-mesh strainer

Medium bowl

Cheesecloth or clean cotton napkin

Large liquid measuring cup or large bowl

Stand mixer with a whisk attachment

Dish towel

Rubber spatula

Small airtight storage container

¡FUERA! Go!

1. Set a fine-mesh strainer over a medium bowl. Lay a triple layer of cheesecloth or a very clean cotton napkin inside the fine-mesh strainer, with the extra hanging over the edge. Set this aside.

2. Combine the water and ice in a large liquid measuring cup and place it in the refrigerator.

3. Add the cream to the bowl of a stand mixer. Lock the bowl into place and attach the whisk attachment to the stand mixer. Cover the mixer with a dish towel to avoid splatters (see photo 1 on page 34).

4. Start the mixer on low speed and whip for 2 minutes. (Do not peek under the towel—the cream will splatter.)

5. Increase the speed to medium and keep whipping for another 2 minutes. (Now you can peek under the towel—the cream will look thicker but still liquid-y.)

6. Increase the speed to high and whip for another 2 minutes. (You can watch now—but do not remove the towel completely.)

7. The cream will form peaks, and suddenly it will get grainy—just keep whipping until the solids (butter) separate from the liquid (buttermilk), about 1 more minute (see photo 2 on page 34). (There will be a bit of splatter, so cover the stand mixer again.) Stop the mixer and remove the bowl.

8. Pour the butter and buttermilk into the cheesecloth-lined strainer. Gather the edges of the cheesecloth, twist tightly, and squeeze (firmly but gently) over the strainer to drain as much buttermilk as possible.

KEEP GOING

9. Discard the buttermilk. Place the butter in the now-empty medium bowl and discard the cheesecloth.

10. Now is the time to wash the butter! Pour half the ice water over the butter until it is covered. Use your hands (or a rubber spatula) to squeeze the butter and remove the excess liquid inside (see photo 3, below)—the water will turn cloudy.

11. Lift the butter out of the water and discard the cloudy water. Place the butter back in the bowl. Pour the remaining ice water over the butter and repeat the washing one more time. (The water should look cleaner.)

12. Place the butter in a small airtight storage container. Gently press the butter with your fingers to evenly pack it inside the container and cover it with the lid. (The butter can be refrigerated for up to 3 weeks.)

CÓMO HACER MANTECA (HOW TO MAKE BUTTER)

I put a dish towel over the stand mixer to avoid splatters. Make sure that it covers the mixer and hangs outside the bowl.

1. Cover the stand mixer with a dish towel to avoid splatters (ask a grown-up for help).

2. The cream will form peaks, and suddenly it will get grainy. Just keep whipping until the solids (butter) separate from the liquid (buttermilk), about 1 more minute.

3. Pour half the ice bath water over the butter until it is covered. Use your hands (or a rubber spatula) to squeeze the butter and remove the excess liquid inside—the water will turn cloudy.

ARGENTINA, EL PAÍS DE LAS VACAS

(ARGENTINA, THE LAND OF COWS)

Argentina is often associated with three things: fútbol (soccer), tango, and . . . cows. Cows? You might be imagining cows roaming freely everywhere, right? But when you grow up on the seventh floor of an apartment building like I did, the closest you'll ever come to a cow is at a fair, behind a fence! For many years, Argentina was the world's top consumer of beef per capita. And the dairy production is pretty great, too. After all, good butter comes from good cream.

MERMELADA DE FRUTILLA
(STRAWBERRY JAM)

 Argentina

MAKES **2 cups**

DIFFICULTY LEVEL

¡EN SUS MARCAS! Ready!

●●●·●●●●●●●●●●●●●

INGREDIENTS

- 2 pounds **strawberries**, hulled and quartered (see page 199)
- ¼ cup **sugar**
- 1 whole **clove**
- Pinch **kosher salt**

¡LISTOS! Set!

●●●●●●●·●●·●●●●·●●●

EQUIPMENT

- Medium saucepan
- Wooden spoon
- Potato masher
- Spoon
- Small plate
- Ladle
- 2 (8-ounce) jars with tight-fitting lids

Growing up, I was lucky to live in the same house as my abuela, so I was always in the kitchen watching her and learning. My abuela often made homemade jams—we never had store-bought. She made jams from all kinds of different fruit—quince, orange, apricot, you name it! But to this day my favorite jam is strawberry. Every year I look forward to strawberry season. My birthday is in October, which happens to be when strawberries are at their best in Argentina. My earliest memories of making jam with my abuela involve huge pots and hours of intense but sweet labor. Over the years I've simplified how I make jam, but it's just as delicious as my abuela's. This is not the kind of jam that will last forever; it goes straight in the refrigerator and stays good for up to three weeks.

1. Place the strawberries in a medium saucepan and sprinkle the sugar evenly over top. Stir gently with a wooden spoon. Let the strawberries sit for 30 minutes.

2. Add the clove and the salt. Cook the strawberries over medium heat, stirring occasionally, for 10 minutes.

3. Turn off the heat and slide the saucepan to a cool burner. Carefully mash the strawberries with a potato masher until the strawberries are mostly broken down (ask a grown-up for help—the mixture will be HOT).

4. Continue to cook the strawberry mixture over medium heat, stirring often, for 10 more minutes. Turn off the heat. Let the jam cool for 2 minutes.

5. Dollop 1 spoonful of jam onto a small plate and place the plate in the refrigerator for 5 minutes. Do the plate test to check for doneness, following the photo below.

6. Let the jam cool completely, about 40 minutes. Remove the clove and discard it. Use a ladle to transfer the jam to two 8-ounce jars. Cover the jars with lids. Refrigerate the jam until it is set, at least 8 hours. Serve. (Jam can be refrigerated for up to 3 weeks.)

CÓMO HACER LA PRUEBA DEL PLATO (HOW TO DO THE PLATE TEST)

Drag your finger through the middle of the jam. If the jam stays divided (and does not run back into the middle), it's done. If the jam is still too runny, return the saucepan to medium heat and continue to cook for 3 more minutes. Then repeat the plate test.

MANGÚ CON LOS TRES GOLPES

(MASHED GREEN PLANTAINS WITH EGGS, CHEESE, AND SALAMI)

Mangú, or boiled and mashed green plantains, could easily be the national dish of the República Dominicana. When served with fried cheese, salame dominicano, and fried eggs, it is called los tres golpes (the three strikes). Three strikes and you're out, as they say—and you will feel full after eating mangú! I tried mangú for the first time on the day I moved to Jersey City, New Jersey. I was very hungry and very tired and had very little money on me. I decided to get some food at the Dominican restaurant down the street from my new apartment and ordered mangú. It did the job—filling my belly plus inspiring me with a new flavor combo. Not to mention: I got to make friends with the people at the little restaurant. Since then, I have had many plates of mangú—often shared with friends, since it is indeed a big breakfast! Mangú is often served with pickled red onions—make the pickled onions ahead of time, as they take a while.

República Dominicana

SERVES **4**

DIFFICULTY LEVEL

¡EN SUS MARCAS!  Ready!

●●●●●●●●●●●●●●●●

INGREDIENTS

MANGÚ

2 **green plantains**, peeled and cut into 2-inch pieces (see the photos on page 41)

1½ teaspoons **kosher salt**

2 tablespoons **unsalted butter**

2 **garlic cloves**, peeled and minced (see page 19)

LOS TRES GOLPES

1 recipe **Cebollas en Vinagre** (page 170)

2 teaspoons **olive oil**

4 slices **queso de freír** or **halloumi cheese**, about ¼ inch thick, patted dry with paper towels

4 slices **salame dominicano** or **Taylor ham**, about ¼ inch thick

1 recipe **Huevos Fritos** (page 166)

¡LISTOS! Set!

●●●●●●●●●●●●●●●●●

EQUIPMENT

Large saucepan	Ladle
Ruler	Liquid measuring cup
Paring knife	
12-inch nonstick skillet	Colander
	Potato masher
Spatula	Oven mitts
Rimmed baking sheet	Cooling rack

¡FUERA!  Go!

●●●●●●●●●●●●●●●●●

1. For the mangú: Place the plantains in a large saucepan. Add enough water to cover the plantains by 1 inch. Add the salt. Bring to a boil over medium-high heat and cook until the plantains are tender but slightly firm and the tip of a paring knife slips easily in and out of the plantains (ask a grown-up for help), about 20 minutes. Turn off the heat.

2. While the plantains cook, adjust an oven rack to the middle position and heat the oven to 200 degrees.

3. For los tres golpes: In a 12-inch nonstick skillet, heat the oil over medium heat for 1 minute (the oil should be hot but not smoking). Add the queso de freír and salame dominicano to the skillet and cook until golden brown, 1 to 2 minutes.

4. Use a spatula to flip the queso de freír and salame and cook until golden brown on the second side and the edges of the cheese start to melt, 1 to 2 minutes. Turn off the heat and slide the skillet to a cool burner.

KEEP GOING

5. Transfer the queso de freír and salame to a rimmed baking sheet and place the baking sheet in the oven to keep them warm.

6. This is a good time to cook the Huevos Fritos in the now-empty skillet.

7. When the plantains are ready, use a ladle to carefully transfer 1 cup of the cooking liquid to a liquid measuring cup (ask a grown-up for help).

8. Put a colander in the sink and ask a grown-up to drain the plantains. Return the drained plantains to the saucepan. Add the butter, garlic, and ½ cup of the reserved plantain cooking water.

9. Carefully mash the plantains with a potato masher until no large pieces remain. Add more cooking water, a little bit at a time, as needed to loosen until it reaches the consistency of mashed potatoes (you might not need all the water). Season the mangú with salt and pepper to taste.

10. Use oven mitts to remove the rimmed baking sheet from the oven and place it on a cooling rack (ask a grown-up for help). Serve the mangú with los tres golpes—queso de freír, salame, and Huevos Fritos—and Cebollas en Vinagre on the side.

❝ IT WAS GOOD! I LIKED THE TEXTURE!"

—Trey, age 10

¿QUÉ ES UN PLÁTANO? (WHAT IS A PLANTAIN?)

Plátanos, or plantains, may look like bananas, but they definitely are not the same thing. Popular in places like Africa and South Asia in addition to Latin America, plantains have thicker peels, a different flavor, and very different uses than the bananas found most often in the United States. Botanically, plantains are part of the banana family of plants, but unlike bananas, plantains are not sold as a bunch and must be thoroughly cooked before you can eat them. Similar to bananas, however, plantains turn from green to yellow to black as they ripen (learn more in "Como Maduran los Plátanos," page 161), and ripe plantains are softer and sweeter. Both green and ripe plantains are used for cooking. Mangú is one of the most popular ways to eat plantains in the República Dominicana, but its cousin, mofongo, in which the plantains are fried before being mashed rather than boiled, is found in Puerto Rico. How else have you tried plantains?

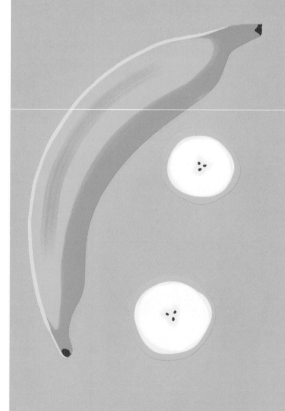

1. Place the plantains on a cutting board. Use a chef's knife to cut off the ends of each plantain.

2. With the plantain on its side, slice along the vein lengthwise (the long way) to split the peel open, making sure not to cut into the fruit.

3. Use a spoon or your hands to peel back the skin from the plantains.

GALLO PINTO
(RICE AND BEANS)

Gallo pinto, which means "spotted rooster," is inspired by the dish's looks: white rice speckled with black beans, like spotted rooster feathers. It is one of the most famous recipes in Costa Rica, and is popular in other countries, such as Nicaragua. My mom visited Costa Rica years ago, and when she came back from that trip, she was so excited to tell me about gallo pinto because she knew how much I love a dish made of leftovers. Salsa Lizano—a smooth brown sauce, sort of like Worcestershire sauce—is made commercially with molasses, cornstarch, and other spices. It is superpopular in Costa Rica and traditionally used in this dish, but personally I am not a huge fan of it, so I often replace it with chicken broth, like I do in this recipe. In Costa Rica, gallo pinto is usually served alongside coffee and warm flour tortillas. What will you eat yours with? This recipe calls for cold white rice. If you do not have any leftover rice, you can cook rice and let it cool completely before using it.

Costa Rica

SERVES 4

DIFFICULTY LEVEL

¡EN SUS MARCAS! Ready!

INGREDIENTS

- 2 tablespoons **olive oil**
- 1 **onion**, peeled and chopped fine (see page 19)
- 1 **small red bell pepper**, stemmed, seeded, and chopped fine (see page 20)
- 2 **garlic cloves**, peeled and chopped (see page 19)
- 1 teaspoon **ground cumin**
- 1 teaspoon **ground coriander**

- 2 cups cooked **white rice**, cooled (or left over) (see Arroz Blanco, page 154)
- 3 tablespoons **chicken** or **vegetable broth**, plus extra as needed
- 1 (15-ounce) can **black beans**, drained but not rinsed (or 1½ cups homemade) (see Frijoles Negros, page 152)

Fresh cilantro leaves

SERVING SUGGESTIONS

You can try one (or all) of these add-ons until you find out which one is your favorite!

Scrambled eggs

Avocado slices (see page 57)

Maduros (see page 160)

Sliced **queso fresco centroamericano** or **feta cheese**

Flour tortillas

¡LISTOS! Set!

EQUIPMENT

12-inch skillet

Wooden spoon

Serving platter

¡FUERA! Go!

1. In a 12-inch skillet, heat the oil over medium-high heat for 1 minute (the oil should be hot but not smoking). Add the onion and cook, stirring a few times with a wooden spoon, until it starts to turn translucent, 3 to 4 minutes.

2. Add the bell pepper and cook until it starts to soften, about 3 minutes.

3. Stir in the garlic, cumin, and coriander. Add the cooled rice (which will probably look like a lump!) and the broth and cook, stirring often to break up the rice, until the rice absorbs the broth, about 3 minutes. If the rice is too dry, add extra broth, a little bit at a time, as needed.

4. Add the beans and cook, stirring gently (you don't want a mushy gallo pinto!), until the beans are warmed through, 5 to 7 minutes.

5. Turn off the heat. Season with salt and pepper to taste. Transfer the gallo pinto to a serving platter and sprinkle with the cilantro leaves. Serve alongside any of the serving suggestions, or try it on its own!

SALTEADO (STIR-FRY)

This is a quick recipe for a stir-fry. The Spanish word for it, "salteado," comes from the verb "saltar," which means "to jump"! It makes a lot of sense, right?

CHILAQUILES VERDES

(TORTILLA CHIPS WITH GREEN SALSA, CHEESE, BEANS, AND FRIED EGGS)

I don't recall where I was or what I was doing the first time I tried chilaquiles—but I do remember the flavor and texture of this perfect dish. The tortillas were still crunchy but covered with a slightly spicy salsa, creamy refried beans, and salty crumbled queso fresco and topped with runny fried eggs. What I've created here is a very approachable version of chilaquiles, one of my favorite recipes

from México, that I hope you make your own! The extra salsa verde can be saved in an airtight container in the refrigerator for up to a week. If you can't find crema, you can use sour cream instead: Thin ½ cup of sour cream with 2 tablespoons of water or 1 tablespoon of water and 1 tablespoon of lime juice.

 México

SERVES **4**

DIFFICULTY LEVEL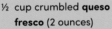

¡EN SUS MARCAS! **Ready!**

INGREDIENTS

SALSA VERDE

1 pound **tomatillos**, husks and stems removed, rinsed well and dried

2 **poblano chiles**

1 **jalapeño chile**

1 **small onion**, peeled and cut into 6 large chunks

3 **garlic cloves**, peeled (see page 19)

½ cup **chicken broth**

1 tablespoon **olive oil**

1 teaspoon **kosher salt**

½ cup **fresh cilantro leaves and stems**

CHILAQUILES

1 (15-ounce) can **refried beans**

2 tablespoons **water**

1 recipe **Huevos Fritos** (optional) (page 166)

8 ounces **tortilla chips**

½ cup crumbled **queso fresco** (2 ounces)

½ cup **crema** (or sour cream—see the note on the left)

½ cup **fresh cilantro leaves**, torn into pieces

¡LISTOS! **Set!**

EQUIPMENT

Rimmed baking sheet

Oven mitts

Cooling rack

Tongs

Blender

Medium bowl

Plastic wrap

Disposable gloves

Dish towel

Small saucepan with a lid

Rubber spatula

Serving platter

Liquid measuring cup

¡FUERA! **Go!**

1. For the salsa verde: Adjust an oven rack to the middle position and heat the oven to 400 degrees. Place the tomatillos, poblanos, jalapeño, onion, and garlic on a rimmed baking sheet.

2. Place the baking sheet in the oven and roast for 20 minutes.

3. Use oven mitts to remove the baking sheet from the oven and place it on a cooling rack (ask a grown-up for help). Increase the oven temperature to 450 degrees. Use tongs to transfer the tomatillos, onion, and garlic to a blender jar and set them aside.

4. Flip the poblanos and jalapeño. Use oven mitts to return the baking sheet to the oven and continue to roast until the chiles are blistered, 20 to 25 minutes.

5. Use oven mitts to remove the baking sheet from the oven and place it on the cooling rack (ask a grown-up for help). Use tongs to transfer the chiles to a medium bowl. Cover the bowl with plastic wrap and set it aside for 10 minutes.

KEEP GOING

6. Meanwhile, add the broth, oil, salt, and ½ cup cilantro to the blender jar.

7. Put disposable gloves on. Uncover the bowl with the chiles. Use your hands to peel, stem, and seed the chiles, following the photos on the right.

8. Place the lid on top of the blender and hold it firmly in place with a folded dish towel. Turn on the blender and process until well combined, 30 seconds to 1 minute. (The salsa verde should be liquid-y, but you should be able to see some tomatillo seeds and tiny green flecks of the rest of the ingredients.)

9. For the chilaquiles: Put the refried beans and water in a small saucepan. Cook over medium-low heat, stirring constantly with a rubber spatula, until the beans are warm, about 5 minutes. Turn off the heat and cover the saucepan with a lid to keep the beans warm.

10. This is a good time to cook the Huevos Fritos (if using).

11. Spread the tortilla chips on a serving platter. Dollop half the refried beans on top, then pour 1½ cups salsa verde all over the chips. Add the remaining refried beans.

12. Sprinkle the queso fresco evenly over top, drizzle with the crema, then sprinkle ½ cup cilantro over top. Place the eggs (if using), sunny-side up, on top. Serve with extra salsa verde. (The extra salsa verde can be refrigerated in an airtight container for up to 1 week.)

TOTOPOS (TORTILLA CHIPS)

The word "totopos," which in Spanish means "tortilla chips," comes from the Aztec or Nahuatl word "totopochtli," which means "something toasted" and "noisy to eat." And that's just what they are! Tortilla chips are made most often from corn tortillas and can be baked or fried to turn them into crunchy chips. Because baking or frying the tortillas removes water, it helps them last longer than fresh tortillas, so there's less waste!

1. Use your hands to peel off the skin of each chile.

2. Split the chiles open with your fingers and remove the stem and seeds. Add the peeled, stemmed, and seeded chiles to the blender jar. Discard all the stems and seeds.

THE SAUCE WAS FRESH, ZESTY, AND DELICIOUS!! DEFINITELY WILL MAKE AGAIN. WE HAVE ALREADY COME UP WITH SEVERAL WAYS TO USE IT."

—Maya, age 13

BALEADAS
(FLOUR TORTILLAS WITH BEANS, CHEESE, AND CHORIZO)

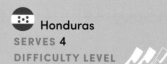 

Honduras

SERVES **4**

DIFFICULTY LEVEL

¡EN SUS MARCAS! Ready!

●●•●●●●●●●••●●●

INGREDIENTS

4 (10-inch) **flour tortillas**

1 pound **Mexican chorizo sausage** (about 4 links), removed from casings and crumbled (see the photos, below right)

1 (15-ounce) can **refried beans**

¼ cup **water**, plus extra as needed

1 **ripe avocado**, halved, pitted, and cut into ½-inch pieces (see page 57)

½ **small red onion**, peeled and sliced thin (see page 19)

½ cup crumbled **queso fresco, feta cheese,** or shredded **block mozzarella cheese** (2 ounces)

¼ cup **crema** (or sour cream—see the note on the left)

¡LISTOS! Set!

●●●●●●●●•●●●●●•●●●

EQUIPMENT

Rimmed baking sheet	Rubber spatula
	Small bowl
Parchment paper	Aluminum foil
Dish towel	Medium saucepan with a lid
Oven mitts	
Cooling rack	
10-inch nonstick skillet	

Baleadas are a popular street dish in Honduras. At their simplest, they're thick wheat-flour tortillas filled with refried beans, queso fresco, and crema and then folded in half. But when I make baleadas, I like to add avocado and crumbled and cooked Mexican chorizo. (If you're feeling adventurous, you can try experimenting and adding other cooked and shredded or crumbled meats, scrambled eggs, or cooked or raw veggies!) Baleadas are often served with curtido (pickled cabbage and carrots) (page 168). If you can't find crema, you can use sour cream instead: Thin ½ cup of sour cream with 2 tablespoons of water or 1 tablespoon of water and 1 tablespoon of lime juice.

1. Adjust an oven rack to the middle position and heat the oven to 350 degrees. Line a rimmed baking sheet with parchment paper and scatter the tortillas on top. Place a second piece of parchment over the tortillas and place a damp dish towel over the parchment. Place the baking sheet in the oven, reduce the temperature to 200 degrees, and bake until the tortillas are warmed through, 3 to 5 minutes. Use oven mitts to transfer the baking sheet to a cooling rack (ask a grown-up for help).

2. Meanwhile, in a 10-inch nonstick skillet, cook the chorizo over medium-high heat, stirring occasionally with a rubber spatula, until browned, 5 to 6 minutes. Turn off the heat. Carefully transfer the chorizo to a small bowl. Cover the bowl with aluminum foil to keep warm.

3. Put the refried beans and water in a medium saucepan. Cook over medium-low heat, stirring constantly with a rubber spatula, until the beans are warm and have a spreadable consistency, about 5 minutes. (Add extra water, a tablespoon at a time, as needed to loosen the beans.) Turn off the heat and cover the saucepan with a lid to keep the beans warm.

4. To assemble your baleadas, divide the refried beans evenly among the tortillas and spread them into an even layer. Top with chorizo, avocado, red onion, and queso fresco, dividing each evenly among the tortillas. Drizzle the crema over top.

5. Fold each tortilla in half. Serve.

CÓMO QUITAR LAS TRIPAS DEL CHORIZO (HOW TO REMOVE CHORIZO CASINGS)

1. Use a chef's knife to trim off 1 end of the chorizo. Then use kitchen shears to snip through the chorizo casing from end to end.

2. Pull the casing off the chorizo and discard the casing.

3. Crumble the chorizo into small pieces.

AREPAS CON QUESO
(CORN CAKES WITH CHEESE)

My first taste of an arepa was as a grown-up living in New York City, at a Venezuelan restaurant in the East Village. I went with friends, and we shared a lot of different kinds of arepas. My favorite on that day was a reina pepiada, a sandwich-like arepa stuffed with shredded chicken, mashed avocado, mayonnaise, and chopped cilantro. The warm arepa tasted slightly sweet from the corn and paired so well with the savory chicken. Since then, I've been on a mission to try as many arepas as possible—and

let me tell you, there are many to try. At its most basic, an arepa is a blank canvas made of masarepa (a precooked corn flour), salt, and water. Different countries specialize in different types of arepas. In Venezuela, arepas are often filled like sandwiches. In Colombia, some varieties are griddled or toasted with cheese or eggs. At home, I make my arepas in the Colombian style and like to fill them with melty cheese or eat them alongside some Huevos Pericos.

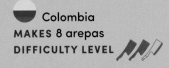
Colombia

MAKES 8 arepas

DIFFICULTY LEVEL

¡EN SUS MARCAS! Ready!

●●●●●●●●●●●●●●●●●

INGREDIENTS

2 cups room-temperature **water**

2 tablespoons **unsalted butter**, melted and cooled

1 teaspoon **kosher salt**

2 cups (10 ounces) **masarepa blanca** (white masarepa) (see "¿Qué es masarepa?" on page 52)

1 cup shredded **gouda cheese** (or any semisoft cheese such as **cheddar** or **block mozzarella**) (4 ounces) (see page 21)

1 recipe **Huevos Pericos** (optional) (page 54)

¡LISTOS! Set!

●●●●●●●●●●●●●●●●●

EQUIPMENT

Medium bowl

Wooden spoon

Dish towel

Ruler

Large plate

12-inch cast-iron skillet or nonstick skillet

Spatula

Rimmed baking sheet

Butter knife

1-tablespoon measuring spoon

Oven mitts

Cooling rack

¡FUERA! Go!

●●●●●●●●●●●●●●●●●●

1. In a medium bowl, combine the room-temperature water, melted butter, and salt. Slowly add the masarepa to the bowl while stirring with a wooden spoon (or go straight in there with your hands—see photo 1 on page 53). Continue mixing until the dough comes together, no dry lumps remain, and the dough releases from the sides of the bowl.

2. Cover the bowl with a dish towel and let the dough rest on the counter for 30 minutes.

3. Adjust an oven rack to the middle position and heat the oven to 350 degrees.

4. Divide the dough into 8 equal portions. Roll 1 portion into a ball. Flatten the ball until you have a disk about 3½ inches wide and ½ inch thick (see photo 2 on page 53) and place the disk on a large plate. Repeat with the remaining dough to make a total of 8 disks of dough.

5. Heat a 12-inch cast-iron skillet over medium-high heat until very hot, about 2 minutes.

KEEP GOING

> **IT TASTED GOOD. THE CHEESE FLAVOR WAS NOT TOO STRONG. IT TASTED LIKE POPCORN."**
>
> —Ethan, age 7

¿QUÉ ES MASAREPA?
WHAT IS MASAREPA?

Corn flour is a very important ingredient in Latin American cuisine—but there is more than one kind. Masa harina is a type of corn flour made by drying and grinding masa dough, which is made from corn that has been nixtamalized, or soaked in an alkaline solution to change both its flavor and structure. Masa harina is used to make corn tortillas. Arepas, however, are made with a particular kind of corn flour called masarepa. To make masarepa, corn is precooked and then ground. Before 1960, when the first commercial version became available, cooks needed to go through a very laborious process of cleaning, grinding, cooking, and milling corn to make masarepa. Being able to buy ready-to-use masarepa makes cooking these arepas so much easier!

6. Place 4 disks of dough in the skillet and cook until spotty brown, about 5 minutes. Use a spatula to flip the arepas and continue to cook until spotty brown on the second side, about 5 more minutes. They should look dry, with some brown spots.

7. Transfer the arepas to a rimmed baking sheet. Repeat cooking with the remaining 4 disks of dough.

8. Split each arepa in half using a butter knife (ask a grown-up for help—the arepas will be HOT!). Fill each arepa with 2 tablespoons gouda and close them.

9. Place the baking sheet in the oven and bake until the cheese is melted, about 3 minutes. Use oven mitts to remove the baking sheet from the oven and place it on a cooling rack (ask a grown-up for help). Let the arepas cool slightly, about 2 minutes. Serve with Huevos Pericos, if desired.

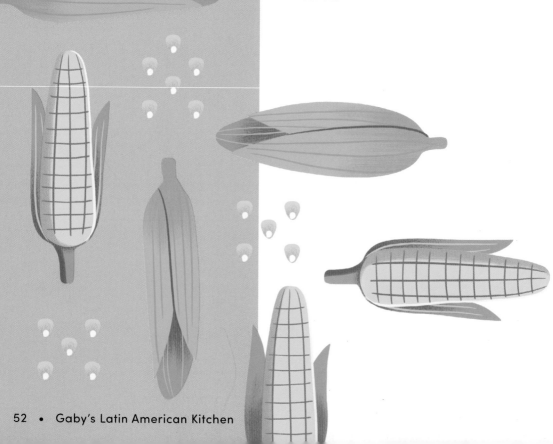

There is no risk of overmixing this dough. Masarepa is made of corn and has no gluten, the proteins that create structure in wheat doughs and get tough if mixed too much! To mix with your hands, make a bear-claw shape with your fingers and stir clockwise until the dough releases from the sides of the bowl.

1. In a medium bowl, combine the room-temperature water, melted butter, and salt. Slowly add the masarepa to the bowl while stirring with a wooden spoon (or go straight in there with your hands!). Continue mixing until the dough comes together, no dry lumps remain, and the dough releases from the sides of the bowl.

2. Divide the dough into 8 equal portions. Roll 1 portion into a ball. Flatten the ball until you have a disk about 3½ inches wide and ½ inch thick and place the disk on a large plate. Repeat with the remaining dough to make a total of 8 disks of dough.

HUEVOS PERICOS
(SCRAMBLED EGGS WITH SCALLIONS AND TOMATOES)

I love eggs. I love scallions. And I love tomatoes. Imagine my delight when I learned my friends from Colombia have a name for this combo! "Huevos pericos" translates as "parakeet eggs," which, I'm guessing, is for the bird's (and this dish's) vibrant colors. Huevos pericos can be eaten alone, but they are traditionally served with arepas. (I like to open the arepa and scoop some inside—but you can also just have one bite of eggs and follow with a bite of arepa!)

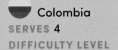 **Colombia**

SERVES **4**

DIFFICULTY LEVEL

INGREDIENTS

- 2 tablespoons **olive oil**
- 2 **tomatoes**, cored and chopped into ½-inch pieces (see page 67)
- 4 **scallions**, the root ends trimmed and the scallions chopped fine
- 4 **large eggs**, cracked into a bowl and beaten with a fork

EQUIPMENT

10-inch nonstick skillet

Rubber spatula

Serving platter

1. Heat the oil in a 10-inch nonstick skillet over medium-high heat for 1 minute (the oil should be hot but not smoking). Add the tomatoes and scallions and cook, stirring occasionally with a rubber spatula, until the tomatoes start to break down and the scallions soften a bit, about 3 minutes.

2. Pour the beaten eggs into the skillet and let the eggs set (no stirring!) for 30 seconds. Then stir until the eggs start to clump up around the scallions and tomatoes but are still slightly wet, about 1 minute. Turn off the heat and slide the skillet to a cool burner.

3. Transfer the egg mixture to a serving platter. Season the eggs with salt and pepper to taste. Serve.

PAN CON PALTA

(BREAD WITH AVOCADO)

Chile

SERVES **4**

DIFFICULTY LEVEL

¡EN SUS MARCAS! Ready!

INGREDIENTS

- 2 **ripe avocados**
- 2 tablespoons **lemon juice**, squeezed from 1 lemon (see page 20)
- 2 tablespoons **olive oil**
- 4 slices **hearty white sandwich bread** (toasted if desired)

¡LISTOS! Set!

EQUIPMENT

- Cutting board
- Chef's knife
- Spoon
- Medium bowl
- Fork

Pan con palta, or avocado on toast, is for Chilean kids what peanut butter on toast is for American kids. My Chilean friend and neighbor Nicole started giving her kids pan con palta before they could even walk! Don't forget the lemon juice: It gives a ton of flavor and helps keep the avocado from going brown.

1. Place the avocados on a cutting board. Use a chef's knife to cut each avocado in half lengthwise (the long way) around the pit, then remove the pits and scoop the flesh from the skin into a medium bowl, following the photos below.

2. Add the lemon juice and oil to the bowl and mash the avocados with a fork until they're as chunky or smooth as you like. I like my avocado mashed but a bit chunky.

3. Season with salt and pepper to taste. Spread the avocado mixture evenly over each slice of bread with a spoon. Serve.

CÓMO ABRIR UNA PALTA (HOW TO OPEN AN AVOCADO)

1. Place the avocados on a cutting board. Use a chef's knife to cut each avocado in half lengthwise (the long way) around the pit.

2. Twist both halves in opposite directions to separate them.

3. Remove the pits (seeds) with a spoon. Discard the pits.

4. Use a spoon to scrape the avocados' flesh out of the skins and transfer it to a bowl (or a cutting board for slicing or chopping).

Almuerzo
Lunch

LLAPINGACHOS (POTATO CAKES)

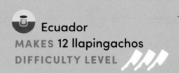

Ecuador
MAKES **12 llapingachos**
DIFFICULTY LEVEL

¡EN SUS MARCAS! Ready!

●●•●●●●●●●●•●●●

INGREDIENTS

- 2 pounds **russet potatoes**, peeled and cut into 1-inch pieces
- 1 tablespoon plus ½ teaspoon **kosher salt**, measured separately
- 5 tablespoons **olive oil**
- 1 **small onion**, peeled and chopped fine (see page 19)
- 2 teaspoons **paprika**
- ½ cup shredded **mozzarella cheese** (2 ounces) (see page 21)

SERVING SUGGESTIONS

Curtido (page 168)

Chopped avocado (see page 57)

Hot sauce

Huevos Fritos (page 166)

¡LISTOS! Set!

●●●●●•●●•●●●●●•●●●

EQUIPMENT

Large saucepan	Potato masher
Paring knife	Plastic wrap
Measuring spoons	¼-cup dry measuring cup
12-inch nonstick skillet	
Rubber spatula	Ruler
2 bowls (1 medium, 1 small)	Rimmed baking sheet
Paper towels	Spatula
Colander	Serving platter

Indigenous peoples living in the Andes mountains, which run down the western side of South America, including Ecuador, have been cultivating potatoes for thousands of years. Even today, thousands of potato varieties are grown across Latin America. I love potatoes in any shape and size, and I picked this dish because it shows one of the many different ways you can prepare them. In llapingachos, you first boil the potatoes until they're tender. Then you mash them, mix them with a few other ingredients, and fry them into little cakes that are crispy on the outside and soft on the inside. Potatoes can be difficult to prep—because they're starchy, they can easily stick to your knife. Be sure to ask a grown-up to help you cut them.

1. Put the potatoes in a large saucepan. Add water to cover the potatoes by 1 inch. Add 1 tablespoon of salt. Bring to a boil over medium-high heat. Cook until the potatoes are tender and cooked through, 10 to 15 minutes (you can check for doneness by piercing the potatoes with the tip of a paring knife—the knife should slide easily in and out of the potatoes; ask a grown-up for help).

2. While the potatoes cook, heat 2 tablespoons of oil in a 12-inch nonstick skillet over medium-high heat for about 1 minute (the oil should be hot but not smoking). Add the onion and paprika and cook, stirring occasionally with a rubber spatula, until the onion is softened, about 5 minutes. Turn off the heat. Transfer the onion mixture to a small bowl. When cool, wipe the skillet clean with paper towels.

3. Place a colander in the sink. When the potatoes are ready, ask a grown-up to drain the potatoes. Transfer the potatoes to a medium bowl. Use a potato masher to mash the potatoes until they are all broken up.

4. Add the onion mixture and the remaining ½ teaspoon of salt and gently stir with a rubber spatula until well combined. Cover the bowl with plastic wrap and let the potato mixture cool on the counter for 30 minutes.

5. Fill and shape 12 llapingachos following the photos below. Place the baking sheet in the refrigerator and chill for 1 hour.

6. In the now-empty skillet, heat 1 tablespoon of oil over medium-high heat for about 1 minute (the oil should be hot but not smoking). Place 4 llapingachos in the skillet. Cook until they are golden brown on the first side, about 2 minutes.

7. Use a spatula to carefully flip the llapingachos—be careful; they are delicate! Cook until the second side is golden brown, about 2 minutes. Transfer the llapingachos to a serving platter.

8. Repeat cooking in 2 more batches, adding 1 more tablespoon of oil to the skillet for each batch. Turn off the heat. Serve the llapingachos with Curtido, chopped avocado, hot sauce, and/or Huevos Fritos.

CÓMO FORMAR LOS LLAPINGACHOS (HOW TO SHAPE LLAPINGACHOS)

1. Scoop ¼ cup of the potato "dough" and use your hands to form it into a 2-inch ball. Make a hole in the middle with your finger. Put 1 heaping teaspoon of mozzarella inside and pinch the hole closed with your fingers.

2. Pat the dough in your hands into a 3-inch circle (like the shape of a hamburger!), and place it on a rimmed baking sheet. Repeat with the remaining potato dough and cheese to make 12 llapingachos.

PUPUSAS
(CORN CAKES WITH BEAN AND CHEESE FILLING)

Pupusas are thick corn cakes filled with savory ingredients, such as cheese, beans, or meat, and cooked on a griddle—think of them as cousins of arepas (page 50) or gorditas. They are especially popular in El Salvador. I ate pupusas for the first time when I was driving near my home in Jersey City and saw a restaurant called La Pupusa Loca (The Crazy Pupusa). Of course I had to stop. After my first bite, I knew I had to learn how to make them myself. It took a few years, but I finally made a friend from El Salvador who could teach me! This recipe is for simple pupusas filled with cheese and beans. Serve them with a side of Curtido (page 168).

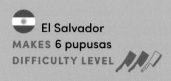 El Salvador

MAKES **6 pupusas**

DIFFICULTY LEVEL

¡EN SUS MARCAS! Ready!

INGREDIENTS

2 cups (8 ounces) **masa harina**

1 teaspoon **kosher salt**

1⅓ cups room-temperature **water**, plus extra if needed

¾ cup shredded **mozzarella cheese** (3 ounces) (see page 21)

¾ cup canned **red kidney beans**, rinsed

1 tablespoon plus 1 tablespoon **vegetable oil**, measured separately

¡LISTOS! Set!

EQUIPMENT

Scissors

Large zipper-lock plastic bag

2 bowls (1 medium, 1 small)

Plate

Clean dish towel or plastic wrap

Ruler

Measuring spoons

Clear pie plate or 8-inch square baking dish

12-inch nonstick skillet

Spatula

Serving platter

¡FUERA! Go!

1. Use scissors to cut along the side seams of a large zipper-lock plastic bag, leaving the bottom seam intact (see photo 1 on page 65). (Your bag will open like a book!)

2. Put the masa harina and salt in a medium bowl and mix well with your hands. Slowly add the room-temperature water to the bowl and mix with your hands until you have a moist, soft dough.

3. Make a golf ball–size ball of dough and gently press it flat. If many large cracks form around the edges, the dough is too dry. Stir in more room-temperature water into the bowl of dough, 1 teaspoon at a time, until the dough no longer cracks when you press it.

4. Divide the dough into 6 equal portions, roll each one into a ball, and place on a plate. Cover with a clean dish towel.

5. In a small bowl, combine the mozzarella and beans.

KEEP GOING

6. Shape and fill 1 pupusa following photos 2–4 on the right. Repeat shaping and filling with the remaining dough and cheese and bean mixture to make 5 more pupusas (there should be 6 total).

7. In a 12-inch nonstick skillet, heat 1 tablespoon of oil over medium heat for about 1 minute (the oil should be hot but not smoking). Swirl the skillet so that the oil covers the bottom evenly. Add 3 pupusas and cook until they are browned on the first side, 3 to 4 minutes.

8. Use a spatula to flip the pupusas. Cook until they are browned on the second side and cooked through, 3 to 4 minutes.

9. Transfer the pupusas to a serving platter. Add the remaining 1 tablespoon of oil to the skillet and repeat cooking with the remaining 3 pupusas. Turn off the heat. Serve the pupusas warm.

1. Use scissors to cut along the side seams of a large zipper-lock plastic bag, leaving the bottom seam intact. Your bag will open like a book!

2. Pat 1 dough ball into a 4-inch-wide circle in your hands. (If the dough is sticky, lightly wet your hands to shape the dough.)

3. Put 2 tablespoons of the cheese and bean mixture in the center of the dough circle, and then pull the sides over and pinch the top together. Roll and shape it back into a ball.

4. Open the bag, place the ball in the center of the bag, and fold over the top of the bag. Use a pie plate to flatten the ball into a 4-inch-wide circle. Transfer the pupusa back to the plate and cover with the dish towel.

CEVICHE DE CAMARÓN
(SHRIMP CEVICHE)

 Ecuador

SERVES 6

DIFFICULTY LEVEL

¡EN SUS MARCAS! Ready!

INGREDIENTS

- 6 cups **water**
- 1 pound **frozen peeled and deveined large shrimp** (26 to 30 per pound), thawed
- 1 **small red onion**, peeled and sliced thin (see page 19)
- 1 cup **lime juice**, squeezed from 8 limes (see page 20)
- ⅔ cup **lemon juice**, squeezed from 4 lemons (see page 20)
- ⅔ cup **orange juice**, squeezed from 2 oranges (see page 20)
- ½ teaspoon **mild hot sauce**
- ½ teaspoon **kosher salt**
- 1 **beefsteak tomato** or 2 **small plum tomatoes**, cored and chopped into ½-inch pieces (see the photos on the right)
- ¼ cup chopped **fresh cilantro** (see page 19)

I've never met a ceviche I did not like. This cool and refreshing dish is eaten all over Latin America. Its ingredients vary from country to country and from cook to cook. Most often, ceviche starts with raw fish or shellfish, which is then "cooked" in acidic citrus juice. However my friend Edmundo, who is a great chef, taught me a trick or two about Ecuadorian ceviche, including this recipe that starts with quickly cooking the shrimp in boiling water. Here is my version of ceviche de camarón ecuatoriano. I love the flavor of fresh lime, lemon, and orange juice here, but you can use store-bought juice in a pinch. Serve your ceviche with saltines or a piece of hearty bread so that you can soak up every drop of the sauce.

¡LISTOS! Set!

EQUIPMENT

Large saucepan

Slotted spoon or spider skimmer

Glass serving bowl

Spoon

Plastic wrap

¡FUERA! Go!

●●●○●●○●●●○○●●●●●●

1. In a large saucepan, bring the water to a boil over high heat. Carefully add the shrimp to the boiling water. Turn off the heat. Use a slotted spoon to stir, making sure that all the shrimp are submerged, and let sit until the shrimp are pink, 2 to 3 minutes.

2. Use the slotted spoon to transfer the shrimp to a glass serving bowl. Place the bowl in the refrigerator and chill for 15 minutes.

3. Remove the bowl of shrimp from the refrigerator. Peel off the tails and discard. Add the onion, lime juice, lemon juice, orange juice, hot sauce, and salt. Stir with a spoon until well combined—make sure that the shrimp are submerged in the juices.

4. Cover the bowl with plastic wrap. Place in the refrigerator and chill for at least 30 minutes.

5. When you are ready to serve the ceviche, add the tomato and cilantro and stir to combine. Season with salt to taste. Serve.

¿QUÉ ES EL CEVICHE? (WHAT IS CEVICHE?)

While the exact origins of ceviche are disputed (both Perú and Ecuador claim to have invented the dish), archaeologists believe that thousands of years ago, Indigenous people on the coast of South America were "cooking" fish using different acidic liquids. Today, ceviche is eaten all over Latin America, and it usually consists of fresh raw fish that is marinated in some sort of citrus juice. As the raw fish soaks, acids in the citrus juice "cook" it, firming it up and turning it from translucent to opaque. Even though this Ecuadorian shrimp ceviche starts with cooked shrimp, a 30-minute soak in the citrusy-tomatoey sauce lets the shrimp absorb its flavor. (In Ecuador, ceviche is often served with a topping of crunchy popcorn—fun, no?)

CÓMO QUITARLE EL CORAZÓN DE UN TOMATE (HOW TO CORE A TOMATO)

1. Use a small serrated knife to cut the tomato in half from top to bottom (through the stem).

2. Place each tomato half flat side down. Use the tip of the knife to cut out the core from each half.

SINCRONIZADA
(HAM AND CHEESE QUESADILLA)

I love quesadillas, I really do! They are easy to make and easy to eat. They are my go-to lunch at least once or twice a week. I never ate quesadillas growing up—I learned about them only in my late 20s, thanks to a dear friend from Puebla, México. Every time I visited, he made me ham and cheese quesadillas. It wasn't until later that I learned they are called "sincronizadas," which means "synchronized."

(Why? I've never been able to find out. My best guess: They help synchronize my happiness with the present moment?!) They require only three ingredients and take 10 minutes to make . . . what's not to like?! To make your lunch more interesting, you can serve your sincronizada with salsa, crema, guacamole (page 98), and/or Pico de Gallo (page 172).

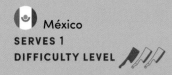 México

SERVES 1

DIFFICULTY LEVEL

¡EN SUS MARCAS! Ready!

INGREDIENTS

- 1 teaspoon **vegetable oil**
- 2 (6-inch) **flour tortillas**
- ¼ cup shredded **mozzarella cheese** (1 ounce) (see page 21)
- 2 slices **deli ham**

  Hot sauce (optional)

¡LISTOS! Set!

EQUIPMENT

10-inch nonstick skillet

Spatula

Plate

Knife

¡FUERA! Go!

1. In a 10-inch nonstick skillet, heat the oil over medium heat for 30 seconds. Place 1 tortilla in the skillet.

2. Sprinkle half the mozzarella evenly over the tortilla. Arrange the ham over the cheese and top with the remaining cheese. Place the remaining tortilla on top and use a spatula to press down on the tortilla.

3. Cook until the cheese starts to melt and the bottom is golden brown, 1 to 2 minutes (you can check by lifting the tortilla a little with the spatula).

4. Use the spatula to flip the sincronizada. Continue to cook until the second side is golden brown, 1 to 2 minutes. Reduce the heat to low and cook until the edges are crispy, 30 to 60 seconds. Turn off the heat.

5. Slide the sincronizada onto a plate. Use a knife to cut it into 4 wedges. Serve with hot sauce (if using).

~~~~~~~~~~~~~~~~~~~~~~~~~~~~~~~~~~~~~~~

¿CON QUESO O SIN QUESO? (WITH CHEESE OR WITHOUT CHEESE?)

While most quesadilla recipes you see have cheese, this ingredient is the source of a big debate in México. The question: Does a quesadilla have to include cheese in order to be called a quesadilla? People who live in Ciudad de México (Mexico City) say no: There, quesadillas are filled with everything from meat to mushrooms to vegetables to herbs—if you want yours with cheese, you might need to order it "con queso" ("with cheese"). In other places, however, people can't imagine quesadillas without cheese! What do you think?

"THE MELTED CHEESE WAS GOOD WITH THE HAM. I LIKED THE CRISPY CRUST!"

—Addison, age 8

SÁNDWICH DE MILANESA DE POLLO
(BREADED CHICKEN SANDWICH)

I could write a poem or a song or even create a monument in honor of my love of milanesas, but believe it or not, those already exist! Instead, I will give you a recipe. For many children in Argentina, there are three phrases that always mean happiness and excitement: "recreo largo," or the longest break between periods in school; "vacaciones," or vacation; and—you guessed it—"sándwich de milanesa"! I, too, loved recreo largo and vacaciones, but it was always a happy day in my house when my mom cooked these breaded, fried chicken sandwiches, and now you can make them for your family. This recipe involves frying, so make sure that you have a grown-up close by to help.

Argentina

SERVES 4

DIFFICULTY LEVEL ▰▰▰

¡EN SUS MARCAS! Ready!
●●•●•●●●●●●••●●●

INGREDIENTS

- 3 **large eggs**
- 1 teaspoon **dried oregano**
- 1 teaspoon **dried parsley**
- ¼ teaspoon **garlic powder**
- ⅛ teaspoon **pepper**
- ⅛ teaspoon **red pepper flakes** (optional)
- ½ teaspoon plus 1 teaspoon **kosher salt**, measured separately
- 4 (3- to 4-ounce) **chicken cutlets**, about ½ inch thick
- 2 cups **plain bread crumbs**
- ½ cup **vegetable oil** for frying
- 8 slices **hearty white sandwich bread**
- ¼ cup **mayonnaise**
- ¼ cup **yellow mustard**
- 4 **leaves green** or **red leaf lettuce**, sliced thin
- 2 **beefsteak tomatoes**, cored and sliced (see page 67)

¡LISTOS! Set!
●●●●●●••●●●●●●•●●●

EQUIPMENT

Medium bowl	Paper towels
Whisk	12-inch skillet
Large shallow dish	Cutting board
Tongs	Butter knife
Large plate	1-tablespoon measuring spoon
Rimmed baking sheet	
	Chef's knife

¡FUERA! Go!
●●●•●●•●●•●●●●●●••●●●●

1. In a medium bowl, whisk the eggs until they are well combined and completely yellow. Add the oregano, parsley, garlic powder, pepper, pepper flakes (if using), and ½ teaspoon salt and whisk to combine.

2. Sprinkle the remaining 1 teaspoon salt evenly over both sides of each piece of chicken. Add the chicken to the egg mixture, making sure that the chicken is submerged. Wash your hands well!

3. Put the bread crumbs in a large shallow dish. Create a "breading assembly line" and bread the chicken following the photos on page 72.

4. Wash your hands and discard any extra egg mixture and bread crumbs—and clean up the counter if you made a mess!

5. Line a rimmed baking sheet with a triple layer of paper towels, and place it near the stovetop. In a 12-inch skillet, heat the oil over medium-high heat for about 2 minutes (the oil should be hot but not smoking).

KEEP GOING

6. Ask a grown-up to help fry the chicken following the photos on the right. Turn off the heat. (Let the oil cool completely before discarding it.)

7. Now it is time to make the milanesa sandwiches! Place the bread on a cutting board. Use a butter knife to spread 4 slices of bread with 1 tablespoon of mayonnaise each. Then spread 1 tablespoon of mustard on each of the remaining 4 slices of bread. Layer each sandwich with lettuce, chicken, and tomato. Use a chef's knife to cut the milanesa sandwiches in half. Serve.

CÓMO EMPANAR EL POLLO (HOW TO BREAD THE CHICKEN)

Milanesas are amazing, but I'll be the first to admit that the breading process can be messy. To keep things as clean and organized as possible, work in an assembly line: Line up your bowl of egg mixture, the shallow dish of bread crumbs, and a large plate, right in a row. This will make it easier to transfer the chicken from the egg mixture to the bread crumbs and then to the plate. Keep in mind that you're working with raw chicken, so be sure to wash your hands often and wash anything the raw chicken touched with hot, soapy water.

1. Use tongs to lift 1 piece of chicken out of the egg mixture, letting the extra egg drip off for 5 seconds over the bowl (don't let the egg drip all over the counter!).

2. Place the chicken in the bread crumbs and use your hand to gently press the bread crumbs on the chicken. Flip the chicken and repeat pressing the bread crumbs on the chicken—I like to do it twice per side. Transfer the breaded chicken to the large plate. Repeat breading with the remaining chicken.

These steps involve frying, so it's very important to make sure that you have a grown-up there to help!

1. Use tongs to carefully add 2 pieces of breaded chicken to the skillet, laying the chicken in the skillet away from you—the oil will be very HOT. Cook until the edges start to turn golden brown, about 2 minutes.

2. Ask a grown-up to carefully use tongs to flip the chicken, again making sure to flip the piece of chicken away from you to avoid any oil splattering toward you. Cook until dark-brown spots appear, 2 to 3 minutes. Transfer the chicken to the paper towel–lined baking sheet. Repeat cooking with the remaining chicken.

 THIS WAS MY FIRST TIME FRYING SOMETHING AND I WAS SURPRISED HOW EASY IT WAS TO MAKE THIS AT HOME."

—Zach, age 10

ARROZ CHAUFA
(PERUVIAN FRIED RICE)

 Perú

SERVES 4

DIFFICULTY LEVEL

¡EN SUS MARCAS! Ready!

●●•○●○●●●●●●•○●●●

INGREDIENTS

- 2 cups cooked **white rice**, cooled (or left over) (see Arroz Blanco, page 154)
- 2 tablespoons **vegetable oil**
- 4 **beef hot dogs**, sliced crosswise (the short way) into ¼-inch-thick pieces
- 5 **scallions**, the root ends trimmed and the white and green parts separated and sliced thin
- 1 **small red bell pepper**, stemmed, seeded, and chopped fine (see page 20)
- 2 **garlic cloves**, peeled and minced (see page 19)
- 1 teaspoon grated **fresh ginger** (see the photos on the right)
- 2 **large eggs**, cracked into a bowl and lightly beaten with a fork
- 2 tablespoons **soy sauce**, plus extra for seasoning

¡LISTOS! Set!

●●●●●●●●○●●●●●●○●●●

EQUIPMENT

12-inch nonstick skillet

Rubber spatula

Serving platter

When I was growing up, my mom always joked that I loved to eat rice with a side of rice. What can I say? I love rice! This multicultural version of fried rice, called arroz chaufa, is a recipe I first learned about from a Peruvian roommate I had here in New Jersey. I make it when I'm very hungry but don't know what to eat. The best part is that you can easily customize it with whatever protein you have on hand. Personally, I love hot dogs!

¡FUERA! Go!

●●○●○●○○●○●○○●●○●●●○●

1. In a 12-inch nonstick skillet, heat the oil over medium heat for about 1 minute (the oil should be hot but not smoking). Add the hot dogs, scallion whites, and bell pepper and cook, stirring with a rubber spatula, for 1 minute.

2. Stir in the garlic and ginger and cook for 1 minute. Push the mixture to 1 side of the skillet.

3. Pour the beaten eggs into the empty side of the skillet and cook, stirring the eggs constantly, until the eggs are no longer wet, about 2 minutes. Stir the eggs into the vegetables and hot dogs.

4. Add the cooled rice (which will probably look like a lump, so break it up with the rubber spatula!) and the soy sauce and stir it into the rest of the ingredients. Cook for 2 more minutes and stir one last time. Turn off the heat.

5. Transfer the arroz chaufa to a serving platter. Sprinkle the scallion greens over top. Season with extra soy sauce to taste. Serve.

CUANDO CHINA SE ENCUENTRA CON PERÚ (WHEN CHINA MEETS PERU)

The word "chaufa" comes from the Cantonese word "chaofan," which translates as "fried rice." In the 1800s, more than 100,000 Chinese immigrants arrived in Perú, many to work in mines and fields and build railroads. They brought cooking techniques and recipes from home, but they didn't always have the same ingredients available in their new country. As a result, they started to improvise, using what was available in Perú. At the same time, these immigrants also introduced some of their traditional ingredients, such as ginger and soy sauce, to Peruvians. Over time, a whole new cuisine—called "chifa"—was born. Chifa combines ingredients and cooking techniques from both cultures. Some popular chifa dishes are lomo saltado (stir-fried beef with vegetables, including potatoes); tallarín con pollo (yellow egg noodles with chicken); and, of course, arroz chaufa. If you were to visit Perú today, especially its capital city of Lima, you'd find chifa restaurants in just about every neighborhood.

CÓMO PELAR Y RALLAR JENGIBRE (HOW TO PEEL AND GRATE GINGER) 〰〰〰

1. Use the side of a small spoon to scrape the skin from about 1 inch of 1 end of a large piece of ginger.

2. Rub the peeled ginger back and forth against the surface of a rasp grater.

CACHAPAS (CORN PANCAKES)

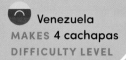 **Venezuela**

MAKES **4 cachapas**

DIFFICULTY LEVEL

¡EN SUS MARCAS! Ready!

●●●●●●●●●●●●●●●●

INGREDIENTS

- 2 cups **frozen corn**, thawed
- ¼ cup **water**
- ¼ cup **fine yellow cornmeal, corn flour, or masarepa**
- ¼ cup **all-purpose flour**
- 1 **large egg**
- 1 tablespoon **sugar**
- ½ teaspoon **kosher salt**
- 4 teaspoons **vegetable oil**
- ½ cup shredded **mozzarella cheese** (2 ounces) (see page 21)
- **Hot sauce** (optional)

¡LISTOS! Set!

●●●●●●●●●●●●●●●●

EQUIPMENT

- Blender
- Dish towel
- Rubber spatula
- Medium bowl
- Measuring spoons
- 8-inch nonstick skillet
- Ladle
- Ruler
- Spatula
- Serving platter

Cachapas are savory-sweet pancakes made of corn, crispy on the outside and tender on the inside—a traditional street food in Venezuela (and one of my absolute favorites!). They are typically eaten with queso de mano, which is a savory Venezuelan fresh cheese, or just with butter. Venezuelans cook cachapas in a budare, a clay or iron plate, similar to a griddle. I first tried cachapas with five of my Venezuelan friends in Journal Square, New Jersey. When I asked how to make them, every one of my friends told a story about how their mother or abuela would make cachapas from scratch, but no one would share their recipe with me! So this recipe is my own interpretation of cachapas, after many, many tries. I love my cachapas with mozzarella cheese and a tiny bit of hot sauce, but you can also try them with spicy mayo, sliced avocado, a different cheese, or even a salad. Try different combinations until you find your favorite!

1. Put the corn, water, cornmeal, all-purpose flour, egg, sugar, and salt in a blender jar. Place the lid on top of the blender and hold the lid firmly in place with a folded dish towel. Turn on the blender. Process for 30 seconds. Stop the blender.

2. Use a rubber spatula to scrape down the sides of the blender jar, making sure that all the cornmeal and flour gets wet. Re-cover the blender with the lid and dish towel. Turn on the blender and process until the mixture looks like wet sand, about 30 seconds. Stop the blender.

3. Pour the batter into a medium bowl, using the rubber spatula to scrape out all the batter.

4. Heat 1 teaspoon of oil in an 8-inch nonstick skillet over medium heat for 30 seconds. Use a ladle to pour one-fourth of the batter (about ⅓ cup) into the skillet. Use the back of the ladle to spread the batter into 5-inch round pancake-like shape.

5. Cook until the bottom is golden brown, about 2 minutes. Use a spatula to flip the cachapa. Cook until the second side is golden brown, 1 to 2 minutes.

6. Transfer the cachapa to a serving platter. Sprinkle 2 tablespoons of mozzarella over top and fold the cachapa like a taco so that the cheese melts.

7. Repeat cooking with the remaining oil and batter to make 3 more cachapas in 3 batches, sprinkling each with 2 tablespoons of cheese. Turn off the heat. Serve the cachapas warm with hot sauce (if using).

MISMA IDEA, NOMBRES DIFFERENTES (SAME IDEA, DIFFERENT NAMES)

Cachapas, arepas, pupusas, gorditas. They might seem similar—they are all made from corn and typically served with fillings or toppings. But these four corn cakes are also quite different: Venezuelan cachapas include fresh corn kernels. They are on the thinner side, and they're typically folded in half around a filling (if they have a filling at all). Arepas (page 50), popular in both Colombia and Venezuela, are made from masarepa (flour made from cooked and ground corn; see page 52). They're cooked on a griddle and then split in half, ready to be filled like a sandwich, or topped with different ingredients. Pupusas (page 62), a favorite in El Salvador, are made with masa harina (a different kind of corn flour created by drying and grinding masa dough; see page 52) and are filled before they are cooked on a hot griddle. Mexican gorditas are also made with masa harina, but they're often fried instead of griddled. They puff as they cook, and then they're split open and stuffed with different fillings.

BUÑUELOS DE ACELGA

(SWISS CHARD FRITTERS)

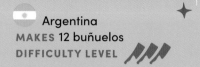 Argentina

MAKES 12 buñuelos

DIFFICULTY LEVEL ///

¡EN SUS MARCAS! Ready!
●●●·●·●●●●●●●··●●●

INGREDIENTS

- 2 pounds **Swiss chard**
- 2 **large eggs**
- 2 tablespoons **all-purpose flour**
- 2 tablespoons **milk**
- ½ teaspoon **kosher salt**
- ¼ teaspoon **pepper**
- ⅛ teaspoon grated **fresh nutmeg** or pinch **ground nutmeg**
- 1 cup **vegetable oil** for frying

¡LISTOS! Set!
●●●●·●●●●·●●●●●·●●●

EQUIPMENT

- 2 bowls (1 large, 1 medium)
- Dutch oven
- Colander
- Rubber spatula
- Cutting board
- Chef's knife
- Ruler
- Rimmed baking sheet
- Paper towels
- 10-inch skillet
- Soupspoon
- Fork
- Slotted spoon

As a kid, I was known for staring at clouds for long periods of time. (To be honest, this is something I still do!) I love clouds, and these buñuelos remind me of them. Buñuelos de acelga are what clouds would look like if they were green (and delicious)! I ate these fritters often growing up—they're a quick and easy lunch and a tasty way to eat your greens. You can use 10 ounces of frozen Swiss chard or spinach, thawed and squeezed in a clean dish towel, instead of the fresh Swiss chard. This recipe involves frying, so make sure that you have a grown-up close by to help!

1. Hold the end of 1 chard stem in one hand. Pinch the thumb and index finger of your other hand on either side of the stem. Slide your hand down the length of the stem, from the bottom to the top, to strip the leaf from the stem. Repeat with the remaining chard (save the stems for another use). Fill a large bowl in the sink with water. Add the chard leaves and swish to remove any dirt. Drain and repeat washing the chard 2 more times.

2. Shake the chard leaves to remove excess water and place them in a Dutch oven. Cook over medium heat until the leaves are soft and wilted, 3 to 4 minutes. Turn off the heat.

3. Place a colander in the sink. Drain the chard in the colander (ask a grown-up for help). Use a rubber spatula to press on the chard leaves in the colander and squeeze as much liquid out of them as possible. Let the chard cool completely, about 15 minutes.

4. Use your hands to squeeze the chard one more time to remove any remaining liquid. Transfer the cooled chard to a cutting board. Use a chef's knife to chop the chard into approximate 1-inch pieces.

5. Transfer the chard to a medium bowl. Add the eggs, flour, milk, salt, pepper, and nutmeg. Use the rubber spatula to stir until the batter is well combined. Line a rimmed baking sheet with a triple layer of paper towels and place it on the counter near the stovetop.

6. Add the oil to a 10-inch skillet. Heat over medium-high heat for about 2 minutes (the oil should be hot but not smoking).

7. Ask a grown-up to use a soupspoon to mound about 2 tablespoons of batter in the skillet. Repeat 2 more times, leaving space between the mounds of batter. Cook until the fritters are golden around the edges, 1 to 2 minutes.

8. Use a fork and slotted spoon to carefully flip the fritters following the photo below. Cook until the fritters are golden brown on the second side, 1 to 2 minutes. Transfer the buñuelos to the paper towel–lined baking sheet.

9. Repeat cooking with the remaining batter in 3 more batches to make 12 buñuelos. Turn off the heat. Serve the buñuelos warm.

CÓMO DAR VUELTA LOS BUÑUELOS (HOW TO FLIP BUÑUELOS)

Using both a fork and a slotted spoon gives you more control as you flip the buñuelos, which prevents them from dropping into the hot oil and splattering. Work slowly and be sure to ask a grown-up to help you—the oil is HOT!

COMPLETOS CHILENOS
(CHILEAN HOT DOGS)

I grew up eating hot dogs from the various hot dog stands around the city of Buenos Aires, my hometown. Since then, I've never met a hot dog I didn't like, so imagine how excited I was to learn how the Chileans prepare theirs: topped with mashed avocado, chopped tomatoes, and sauerkraut and drizzled with condiments such as ketchup, mustard, and mayonnaise. ("Completo" means "full" or "complete," and these hot dog buns are filled to the brim!) In Chile, everyone has their favorite combination of completo toppings, so you can pick and choose your favorites here. Fun fact: A completo italiano (Italian hot dog) is topped with mashed avocado, chopped tomatoes, and mayonnaise—displaying the colors of the Italian flag!

 Chile

SERVES **4**

DIFFICULTY LEVEL

¡EN SUS MARCAS!  Ready!

INGREDIENTS

- 1 **ripe avocado**, halved and pitted (see page 57)
- 1 tablespoon **olive oil**
- 4 **hot dog buns**, toasted if desired
- ¼ cup **mayonnaise**
- 4 **hot dogs**
- 2 **plum tomatoes**, cored and chopped into ¼-inch pieces (see page 67)
- ¾ cup **sauerkraut**
- **Ketchup**
- **Mustard**

¡LISTOS!  Set!

EQUIPMENT

- Small bowl
- Fork
- Butter knife
- 10-inch skillet
- Ruler
- Tongs
- Spoon

¡FUERA!  Go!

1. Place the avocado flesh and oil in a small bowl. Use a fork to mash until the avocado is mostly broken down. Season with salt and pepper to taste.

2. Split the hot dog buns open. Use a butter knife to spread the mayonnaise evenly over each bun; set aside.

3. In a 10-inch skillet, add the hot dogs and cover them with water until it measures about ½ inch deep (the hot dogs should be about halfway submerged in the water). Bring to a boil over medium-high heat. When the water starts boiling, cook for 2 minutes. Turn off the heat.

4. Use tongs to transfer 1 hot dog to each hot dog bun. You can top your completo any way you like! I recommend spooning the tomatoes, sauerkraut, and mashed avocado over top. Then, drizzle with ketchup and mustard and serve.

¿CÓMO SE DICE "HOT DOG"? (WHAT DO YOU CALL A HOT DOG?)

There are delicious hot dogs to try across Latin America—and a bunch of different names for them! Here are a few of my favorites: Colombians refer to them as "perros" ("dogs") and might top them with a mix of mayonnaise and ketchup, pineapple sauce, and crumbled potato chips. Brazilians call them "cachorros," which means "puppies" (so cute!), and often top them with ground beef cooked in tomato sauce with peppers and onions, Parmesan cheese, potato sticks, mashed potatoes, and more. Sometimes the cachorros are even cooked in the tomato sauce. Argentineans (and Uruguayans) call them "panchos." In Argentina, you might see panchos topped with mayonnaise, mustard, and chimichurri sauce, while in Uruguay, cheese, corn, and mustard are popular. And Peruvians and Ecuadorians skip the bun and make salchipapas—a combination of "salchicha" ("hot dog") and "papas" ("potatoes")—cut-up hot dogs with french fries.

CHIVITO URUGUAYO
(STEAK, HAM, CHEESE, AND FRIED EGG SANDWICH)

Chivito uruguayo—filled with a thin slice of tender beef, a fried egg, mozzarella cheese, ham, lettuce, and tomato—is comfort food packed into a sandwich. Growing up, many of my friends were from Uruguay, and they introduced me to this special sandwich. There are whole restaurants dedicated to serving chivito, but I think the best

versions are served in the food stands at fútbol (soccer) games. Sandwich steaks can also be called top sirloin steak or sirloin tip steaks. Don't get shaved steak, like for philly cheesesteaks—it will be too thin. Just make sure that what you get is about ¼ inch thick.

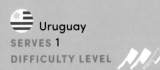 **Uruguay**

SERVES 1

DIFFICULTY LEVEL

INGREDIENTS

Mayonnaise

1 **hamburger bun**

3 (¼-inch-thick) slices **plum tomato**

¼ teaspoon **kosher salt**

1 (4- to 5-ounce) **sandwich steak**
(about ¼ inch thick), often referred to
as top sirloin steak or sirloin tip steak
(see the note on the left)

2 teaspoons **olive oil**

1 **large egg**

1 thick slice **fresh** or **block mozzarella
cheese**

1 slice **deli ham**

1 **romaine lettuce leaf**, cut in half

EQUIPMENT

Butter knife

Paper towels

10-inch nonstick skillet

Tongs

Plate

Spatula

1. Use a butter knife to spread as much mayonnaise as you like over the insides of the hamburger bun. Season the tomato with salt to taste.

2. Pat the steak dry with paper towels. Sprinkle salt evenly over both sides of the steak. Wash your hands.

3. In a 10-inch nonstick skillet, heat the oil over medium-high heat for about 1 minute (the oil should be hot but not smoking). Carefully place the steak in the skillet. Cook for 1 minute. Use tongs to flip the steak and cook for 1 more minute. Transfer the steak to a plate.

4. Add the egg to the skillet and cook for 1 minute. Use a spatula to carefully flip the egg. Turn off the heat.

5. To assemble the sandwich, place the steak on the bottom bun. Then layer on the mozzarella, ham, egg, tomato, and lettuce. Place the top bun on top. Serve while the sandwich is still hot!

¡NO HAY CHIVO EN ESTE SÁNDWICH! (THERE'S NO GOAT IN THIS SANDWICH!)

This sandwich might be called "chivito" ("little goat"), but there is no goat in this recipe. So how did Uruguay's most famous sandwich get its name? The story supposedly goes something like this: In the 1940s, a woman stopped by a restaurant and ordered chivito. But the chef didn't have any goat to serve her—instead he made her a sandwich filled with some of the ingredients he did have on hand, including steak and ham.

TACOS DE CARNE MOLIDA
(GROUND BEEF TACOS)

I love eating with my hands, which is one of the many reasons I love tacos. Tacos were first eaten in México, possibly by Mexican miners, using soft corn tortillas to hold cooked meats. Tacos were reinvented by Mexican Americans in the Southwest and then brought to the masses with fast food options such as Taco Bell. In my taco recipe, I'm going to teach you how to make my version of a very simple carne molida de res (ground beef) filling. There are plenty of topping options, so you can pick and choose what you'd like and make it your very own. ¡Buen provecho! If you can't find crema, you can use sour cream instead: Thin ½ cup of sour cream with 2 tablespoons of water or 1 tablespoon of water and 1 tablespoon of lime juice.

México

MAKES **6 tacos**

DIFFICULTY LEVEL

¡EN SUS MARCAS! Ready!

INGREDIENTS

- 12 (6-inch) **corn tortillas**
- 1 tablespoon **olive oil**
- 1 pound **85 percent lean ground beef**
- 1 tablespoon **ground cumin**
- 2 teaspoons **dried oregano**
- 1 teaspoon **paprika**
- 1 teaspoon **kosher salt**
- ⅛ teaspoon **chili powder** (optional)

TOPPING SUGGESTIONS

Shredded **Mexican cheese blend**

Chopped **fresh cilantro**
(see page 19)

Crema (or sour cream—see the note
on the left)

Pico de Gallo (page 172)

Chopped **avocado** (see page 57)

Hot sauce

¡LISTOS! Set!

EQUIPMENT

Rimmed baking sheet	Cooling rack
Parchment paper	12-inch skillet with lid
Dish towel	
Oven mitts	Wooden spoon

¡FUERA! Go!

1. Adjust an oven rack to the middle position and heat the oven to 350 degrees. Line a rimmed baking sheet with parchment paper and scatter the tortillas on top. Place a second piece of parchment over the tortillas and place a damp dish towel over the parchment. Place the baking sheet in the oven, reduce the temperature to 200 degrees, and bake until the tortillas are warmed through, 3 to 5 minutes. Use oven mitts to transfer the baking sheet to a cooling rack (ask a grown-up for help).

2. While the tortillas warm up, in a 12-inch skillet, heat the oil over medium-high heat for about 1 minute (the oil should be hot but not smoking). Add the beef, breaking it up with a wooden spoon. Cook until the meat is no longer pink, about 5 minutes.

3. Reduce the heat to medium and stir in the cumin, oregano, paprika, salt, and chili powder (if using). Cook, stirring occasionally, until the meat is browned, 3 to 5 minutes. Turn off the heat and cover with a lid to keep warm.

4. Stack the tortillas in piles of two (there should be 6 piles total to make 6 tacos!). Divide the beef mixture among the warm tortillas and top with your favorite toppings! Serve.

¿POR QUÉ DOS TORTILLAS EN UN TACO? (WHY TWO TORTILLAS FOR ONE TACO?)

In México, when you buy tacos on the street, they are usually served with not one but TWO tortillas per taco. Why? It's actually quite simple: because warm, soft corn tortillas tear very easily. After you add all your delicious toppings, inevitably your taco will fall apart! So don't hesitate to double up on your tortillas so that you don't end up eating the taco filling out of your hand!

MEDIALUNA OLÍMPICA

(HAM, CHEESE, AND EGG CROISSANT)

A sándwich olímpico is one of the biggest sandwiches you'll ever see, filled with ham, cheese, lettuce, tomato, peppers, and hard-boiled eggs. In my homage to this classic Uruguayan sandwich, I like to replace the bread with my favorite pastry: a medialuna, which means "half-moon" due to its shape (but here in the United States, you may know it by its French name, croissant!). So here it is, my invention—the Medialuna Olímpica!

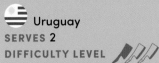 Uruguay

SERVES **2**

DIFFICULTY LEVEL

¡EN SUS MARCAS! Ready!

INGREDIENTS

- 2 **croissants**
- **Mayonnaise**
- ¼ cup **jarred roasted red peppers**
- 2 **Huevos Duros**, peeled and sliced ¼ inch thick (see the recipe on the right)
- 4 slices **deli ham**
- 4 slices **deli Swiss cheese**
- 1 **large romaine lettuce leaf**, cut into ¼-inch-thick strips
- 1 **plum tomato**, cored and sliced ¼ inch thick (see page 67)

¡LISTOS! Set!

EQUIPMENT

Cutting board

Bread knife

Butter knife

¡FUERA!  Go!

1. Place the croissants on a cutting board. Use a bread knife to gently slice each croissant open lengthwise (the long way). Spread as much mayonnaise as you like over the insides of each croissant with a butter knife.

2. You can arrange the ingredients in any way you like, but this is how I do it: Divide the red peppers evenly between the 2 croissants. Layer on the eggs, ham, Swiss cheese, lettuce, and tomato. Season with salt to taste. Close the sandwiches and serve.

HUEVOS DUROS (HARD-BOILED EGGS)

To make Huevos Duros: Fill a medium saucepan with 1 inch of water. Bring the water to a rolling boil over high heat (lots of big bubbles will break the surface of the water). Place **1 to 6 large eggs** in a steamer basket and carefully lower the basket into the saucepan. The eggs can be above or partly under the water. Cover the saucepan, reduce the heat to medium-low, and cook the eggs for exactly 13 minutes. While the eggs cook, combine **2 cups of ice cubes** and **2 cups of cold water** in a medium bowl. Use a slotted spoon to transfer the cooked eggs to the ice bath; let the eggs sit for 15 minutes. Remove the eggs from the ice bath and refrigerate them until you're ready to eat. Crack the eggs against a hard surface (like a counter) and peel away the shells with your hands.

Meriendas y Bebidas
Snacks and Drinks

EMPANADAS DE POLLO
(CHICKEN TURNOVERS)

I grew up eating savory empanadas—pastries filled with different meats, vegetables, and spices; sometimes fried and sometimes baked—made by my family. Each relative used different flavors and ingredient combinations. But the real differentiator between empanada makers was the way they closed the empanadas. Before baking, you need to crimp the dough to keep the filling contained. In Argentina this crimping is called "repulgue," which translates to "hem" or "crimp." My abuela showed me her way of crimping when I was about 8 years old.

It wasn't hard, but I suddenly started doing my own style of repulgue. And not to brag, but I was really good at it! I worked really fast, and the empanadas never burst in the oven. From then on, I was always in charge of crimping. This recipe is my own twist on my mom's version of empanadas de pollo! I simplify things by using frozen empanada dough and rotisserie chicken. If you can't find hojaldradas-style dough rounds, look for packages labeled "para hornear" ("for the oven").

Argentina

MAKES **12 empanadas**

DIFFICULTY LEVEL

¡EN SUS MARCAS! Ready!

INGREDIENTS

- 2 tablespoons **olive oil**
- 1 **onion**, peeled and finely chopped (see page 19)
- 1 **green** or **red bell pepper**, stemmed, seeded, and finely chopped (1 cup) (see page 20)
- ½ teaspoon **kosher salt**
- ½ teaspoon **pepper**
- 2 tablespoons **tomato paste**
- 2 cups shredded **rotisserie** or **leftover chicken** (about 10 ounces)
- 1 cup **chicken broth**
- ½ teaspoon **sweet paprika**
- ½ teaspoon **ground cumin**
- ¼ cup **pitted green olives**, rinsed and chopped
- 1 **large egg**
- 12 (4½-inch) store-bought **hojaldradas-style empanada dough rounds** (see the note on the left)

¡LISTOS! Set!

EQUIPMENT

Medium saucepan with a lid	Parchment paper
Wooden spoon	Fork
Oven mitts	1-tablespoon measuring spoon
3 bowls (1 medium, 2 small)	Dish towel
	Pastry brush
Rimmed baking sheet	Cooling rack

¡FUERA! Go!

1. In a medium saucepan, heat the oil over medium-high heat for about 1 minute (the oil should be hot but not smoking). Add the onion, bell pepper, salt, and pepper and cook, stirring often with a wooden spoon, until the onions just start to brown and peppers are crisp-tender, about 5 minutes.

2. Stir in the tomato paste and cook, stirring and scraping the bottom of the saucepan, until the tomato paste gets darker in color, about 1 minute.

3. Add the shredded chicken, chicken broth, paprika, and cumin and gently stir to combine. Bring to a boil. Reduce the heat to medium, cover the saucepan with a lid, and cook for 6 minutes.

4. Use oven mitts to remove the lid. Gently stir in the olives. Turn off the heat and slide the saucepan to a cool burner. Season with salt to taste. Transfer the chicken mixture to a medium bowl and place it in the refrigerator to cool completely, about 45 minutes.

5. While the filling is cooling, adjust an oven rack to the middle position and heat the oven to 350 degrees. Line a rimmed baking sheet with parchment paper.

KEEP GOING

 VERY YUMMY AND VERY WORTH IT. THE FLAVOR WAS PERFECT. THE FOLDING WAS VERY FUN TO DO."

—Delaney, age 12

6. Fill a small bowl with water. In the second small bowl, lightly beat the egg with a fork. When the filling is cool, fill and shape the empanadas following the photos on the right.

7. Use a pastry brush to paint the tops and sides of the empanadas lightly with the beaten egg. Place the baking sheet in the oven. Bake until the empanadas are golden brown, 35 to 40 minutes.

8. Use oven mitts to transfer the baking sheet to a cooling rack (ask a grown-up for help). Let the empanadas cool for 10 minutes. Serve. (The chicken filling can be frozen for up to 3 months. When you are ready to try your luck with the empanadas, thaw the filling in the refrigerator overnight.)

VAMOS A HABLAR DE LAS EMPANADAS (LET'S TALK ABOUT EMPANADAS)

No one can say exactly where the first empanada was made or eaten, but evidence shows that they originated in a region of Spain called Galicia. The word "empanada" comes from the Galician verb "empanar," which meant "to coat in bread." Brought to Latin America by Spanish colonizers, empanadas come in all kinds of shapes and sizes, with different fillings and breading and cooking methods. They're often savory, but can also be sweet. In Argentina, empanadas can be fried or baked, and the dough is made of wheat flour. There are various types of beef empanadas, some made with ground beef and some made with meat cut in tiny cubes, depending on the region. In Ecuador, they make empanadas de viento ("wind" empanadas). The dough is made of wheat flour and they are filled with quesillo (a type of cheese) and onions and then fried and sprinkled with powdered sugar. In México, the most popular empanadas are fried; made of masa (corn flour); filled with cheese or beef; and served topped with lettuce, pico de gallo, and crema. Every country has their own, and they are amazingly delicious!

I like to create a small assembly line when filling and shaping my empanadas. Some brands of empanada dough will come with a plastic divider to separate the disks of dough. I like to keep the dough on the plastic, using it to help fold the dough, particularly if it's hot in the room where I'm cooking!

1. Place 6 empanada dough rounds on a clean counter. Then place the filling and the water next to them.

2. Place 1 heaping tablespoon of filling in the center of each dough round. Dip your finger in the water, and paint the top edge of each dough round with water in a half-circle shape. Dry your finger on a dish towel.

3. Fold each dough round over, pressing gently on the border to seal the edges. They should look like half moons. Remove and discard the plastic dividers, if you have them.

4. Starting at 1 end, fold the corner of the dough up and over onto the sealed edge. Use your index finger of 1 hand to press down to seal. Hold your index finger in place.

5. With your other hand, stretch and fold the next portion of the edge up and over the tip of your finger. Move your index finger over and press to seal. Repeat along the edge to make a twisted rope shape.

6. Tuck the last corner of the edge underneath the empanada. Place the shaped empanada on the parchment-lined baking sheet. Repeat with the remaining dough and filling.

PICADA ARGENTINA
(ARGENTINEAN-STYLE TAPAS)

 Argentina
SERVES It's up to you!
DIFFICULTY LEVEL

For Argentineans, picada is a reason to gather with friends. It's a reason to hang out with family. Picada is basically a big tray of snacks. You can pick out whatever bites you want! Picada is often served on a tray or cutting board, scattered with all kinds of different things, including cheese; meats; olives; fruits; nuts; and leftovers, such as pieces of Milanesa (page 70). Start by looking around your fridge. What do you see? Any good leftovers?

Then add some cheese, cold cuts, fruits, little canned fishes, potato chips, pretzels, crackers, bread, olives, dried fruits, nuts, or jarred artichokes—the options are quite literally endless . . . and you've got yourself a picada! I have some of my favorites listed to the right, but this picada is all about having fun.

What do you do? Get the biggest cutting board you have, and arrange the cheeses, meats, and anything else you want to include in a beautiful manner. Serve!

CHEESE

I like to have one hard, aged cheese; one tangy, sliceable option; and one creamy option. Some typical cheeses in Argentina are Reggianito, Mar del Plata, and Fresco, but if those are unavailable you can substitute Parmesan, gouda, and Brie.

COLD CUTS

You can pair these sliced meats with cheese and bread, a little bit of sauce, or anything else you like! Try using thinly sliced ham, salami, turkey, or prosciutto.

CANNED FISH

Canned octopus is very popular in Argentina. You can get cans of squid in ink, sardines, or mussels at any gourmet foods store.

NUTS

Something crunchy and salty, such as walnuts, almonds, or peanuts, really brightens up the spread!

BRINED THINGS

I like black olives and green olives, and pickled vegetables of all kinds. You can also look for jars of giardiniera.

BREADY THINGS

Crackers and sliced bread are great, but have you ever tried cheddar cheese on a potato chip? Highly recommend it!

SAUCES

For dipping! Use mayonnaise, mustard, or even leftover Chimichurri (page 174).

FRUIT

You can use fresh or dried fruit. Grapes look great on the tray. I like to add prunes or dates, too.

SOMETHING SWEET

You can use slightly sweet Bizcochitos de Grasa (page 28) or candy—because you always need something sweet!

SOPA PARAGUAYA

(PARAGUAYAN "SOUP" CORNBREAD)

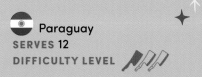

Paraguay

SERVES **12**

DIFFICULTY LEVEL

¡EN SUS MARCAS! **Ready!**

●●●•●●●●●●●●●●●●

INGREDIENTS

2 tablespoons **olive oil**, plus extra for greasing the pan

1 **small onion**, peeled and chopped fine (see page 19)

2½ cups (12 ounces) **fine yellow cornmeal**

1½ teaspoons **kosher salt**

6 **large eggs**, cracked into a bowl and lightly beaten with a fork

2 cups shredded **gouda cheese** (8 ounces) (see page 21)

3 **scallions**, the root ends trimmed and the scallions sliced ½ inch thick (about 1 cup)

1 cup (8 ounces) **milk**

¡LISTOS! **Set!**

●●●●●●●●●●●●●●●●

EQUIPMENT

13-by-9-inch metal baking pan

13-by-9-inch piece of parchment paper

10-inch skillet

Wooden spoon

Large bowl

Oven mitts

Cooling rack

Chef's knife

Legend has it that the first president of Paraguay, Carlos Antonio López, liked to eat a soup made with milk and a little bit of cornmeal. One day his cook added too much cornmeal by mistake, and had to bake it in order for it to finish cooking. Carlos loved the results, however, and immediately dubbed this chewy, casserole-like cornbread "sopa Paraguaya." You can eat your sopa warm or cold. In Asunción, the capital city of Paraguay, it is often served with a glass of tereré, a cold yerba mate drink. Some like to add red and green peppers and fresh corn to their sopa, but I have loved this simpler version ever since my friend Fanni showed me how to prepare it years ago!

1. Adjust an oven rack to the middle position and heat the oven to 375 degrees. Grease a 13-by-9-inch metal baking pan with extra oil. Line the baking pan with parchment paper.

2. In a 10-inch skillet, heat the oil over medium-high heat for about 1 minute (the oil should be hot but not smoking). Add the onion and cook, stirring occasionally with a wooden spoon, until softened, about 5 minutes. Turn off the heat.

3. Transfer the onion to a large bowl (ask a grown-up for help). Add the cornmeal and salt to the bowl and stir with a wooden spoon to combine—it might look messy but you're on the right path!

4. Add the eggs and stir until well combined. Add the cheese and scallions and stir until well combined. Stir in the milk and mix until the mixture resembles thick cake batter.

5. Pour the batter into the greased baking pan and smooth the top. Place the baking pan in the oven and bake until golden brown and set, about 30 minutes.

6. Use oven mitts to transfer the baking pan to a cooling rack (ask a grown-up for help). Let the sopa cool for 5 minutes. Cut into pieces and serve.

ERRORES AFORTUNADOS (LUCKY MISTAKES)

I like to think about recipes that were born out of a mistake, such as Sopa Paraguaya. If Carlos Antonio López hadn't loved that milky soup, and his cook hadn't made a mistake with the cornmeal, would this dish ever have been invented? Another of my favorite stories is about dulce de leche. Legend has it that the cook for an Argentinean politician was cooking milk and sugar but had to leave the kitchen for some reason and forgot all about her pot on the stove. The result? Thick, caramelly, delicious dulce de leche that's now used on all kinds of dishes, including Panqueques con Dulce de Leche (page 200) and Alfajores de Maicena (page 188). Have you ever made a mistake in the kitchen that turned out amazing?

GUACAMOLE CON TOTOPOS

(GUACAMOLE WITH TORTILLA CHIPS)

Guacamole is a dip made of mashed avocados, often mixed with lime juice, cilantro, onions, garlic, olive oil, and spices. I learned to make my version of guacamole from a friend who worked in a Mexican restaurant years ago. She made it for every party she ever held or attended, so I learned from watching and tasting. I like this recipe because it is not spicy—I call it the "friendly" guacamole. (If you like spice, you are welcome to add some finely chopped jalapeño chiles or hot sauce.) Don't forget the totopos!

México

SERVES 6

DIFFICULTY LEVEL

¡EN SUS MARCAS! Ready!

INGREDIENTS

- 3 **ripe avocados**
- ¼ cup **lime juice**, squeezed from 2 limes (see page 20)
- 1 teaspoon **kosher salt**
- 2 **plum tomatoes**, cored and chopped into ½-inch pieces (see page 67)
- ½ cup finely chopped **red onion** (see page 19)
- ¼ cup chopped **fresh cilantro**, plus extra for serving (see page 19)
- 1 tablespoon **olive oil**
- ¼ teaspoon **ground cumin**
- **Tortilla chips**

¡LISTOS! Set!

EQUIPMENT

Cutting board

Chef's knife

Spoon

Medium bowl

Fork

¡FUERA! Go!

1. Place the avocados on a cutting board. Use a chef's knife to cut each avocado in half lengthwise (the long way) around the pit, then remove the pits and use a spoon to scoop the flesh from the skin following the photos on page 57.

2. In a medium bowl, combine the avocados, lime juice, and salt. Use a fork to mash the avocados until broken down but still chunky.

3. Add the tomatoes, onion, cilantro, oil, and cumin and stir gently to combine. Sprinkle with extra cilantro. Serve with tortilla chips. (Guacamole can be covered with plastic wrap pressed directly onto the surface of the guacamole and refrigerated for up to 30 minutes.)

CÓMO EVITAR QUE LOS AGUACATES SE PONGAN MARRONES (HOW TO KEEP AVOCADOS FROM TURNING BROWN)

As you've likely seen, an avocado's bright-green flesh turns brown if it's left exposed to air for too long. And no one likes to eat brown guacamole! What's going on? It's a reaction called oxidation, and it takes place when compounds in the avocado flesh interact with oxygen in the air. To keep your avocado green, you can squeeze a little lime or lemon juice onto any exposed surface (they contain acids that help slow oxidation), or cover your avocado (or guacamole) tightly with plastic wrap to prevent air from touching it. But the best way to avoid brown guacamole? Eat it as soon as it's made!

ELOTES
(CHEESY CORN ON THE COB)

Elote is Mexican-style corn on the cob. It's traditionally served on the street; eaten with your hands; and coated in mayonnaise, salty cotija cheese, chili powder, and a squeeze of fresh lime juice. (Though I love to sprinkle mine with Tajín, a chili-lime seasoning.) Elote is also traditionally cooked on the grill. A few years ago, however, I was teaching cooking classes at a summer camp for kids, where we "traveled" imaginarily around the world through food, learning about "colores y sabores" ("colors and flavors"). One day we landed on this popular street dish from México. We didn't have a grill, so I improvised by boiling the corn and then smearing it with mayo, cheese, and spices. The result was delicious, so now I share it with you!

 México

SERVES **4**

DIFFICULTY LEVEL

¡EN SUS MARCAS! Ready!

INGREDIENTS

- 4 ears **corn**, husks removed
- ¼ cup **mayonnaise**
- ½ cup crumbled **cotija cheese** (2 ounces) or ½ cup grated **Parmesan cheese** (1½ ounces)
- 2 **limes**, cut into quarters
- **Tajín** or **sweet paprika** or **chili powder**
- **Hot sauce** (optional)

¡LISTOS! Set!

EQUIPMENT

Dutch oven

Tongs

Serving platter

Pastry brush

1-tablespoon measuring spoon

¡FUERA! Go!

1. Fill a Dutch oven halfway with water. Bring the water to a boil over high heat.

2. Use tongs to carefully add the corn to the boiling water (ask a grown-up for help). Cook until tender, about 5 minutes. Turn off the heat. Use tongs to transfer the corn to a serving platter. Let the corn cool slightly.

3. Use a pastry brush to brush each ear of warm corn with 1 tablespoon of mayonnaise. Sprinkle each ear with 2 tablespoons cheese, and squeeze 1 lime wedge over top. Sprinkle with Tajín to taste. Drizzle with hot sauce (if using). Serve with remaining lime wedges.

¿QUE ES EL TAJÍN? (WHAT IS TAJÍN?)

Tajín is the name of the company that invented a delicious spice blend that is a mix of dried chiles, dried lime, and salt. While Tajín became popular in México, it is now known and sold all over the world. You can achieve the same flavors by using your own mixture of dried chiles, lime juice, and salt, but tajín is just so easy to use that it's worth seeking out in the grocery store.

MIS NACHOS FAVORITOS
(MY FAVORITE NACHOS)

I love nachos. I love that you eat them with your hands. And that they are versatile. You can make them simple, or add layers of whatever is in your fridge! Nachos are a dish that was born in México but became a staple of Texan-Mexican cuisine, spreading quickly through the United States starting in the 1970s (see more on their history in "¿Quién inventó los nachos?" on the far right).

My nacho recipe is a mix of here and there, but absolutely delicious. My favorite part is the black olives, so don't forget them! If you can't find crema, you can use sour cream instead: For ½ cup sour cream, thin it with 2 tablespoons of water or 1 tablespoon of water and 1 tablespoon of lime juice.

 México

SERVES **6 to 8**

DIFFICULTY LEVEL

¡EN SUS MARCAS! Ready!

INGREDIENTS

- 12 ounces **tortilla chips** (about 1 bag)
- 1 pound **shredded Mexican cheese blend** (4 cups)
- 1 (15-ounce) can **black beans**, drained and rinsed (or 1½ cups homemade) (see Frijoles Negros, page 152)
- ½ cup sliced **black olives**
- ¼ cup sliced **jarred jalapeño chiles**
- 1 **ripe avocado**, halved, pitted, and mashed with a fork (see page 57)
- 3 **plum tomatoes**, cored and chopped into ½-inch pieces (see page 67)
- ½ cup **crema** (or sour cream—see the note on the left)
- 1 cup coarsely chopped **fresh cilantro** (see page 19)

¡LISTOS! Set!

EQUIPMENT

Rimmed baking sheet

Oven mitts

Cooling rack

Tongs

¡FUERA!  Go!

1. Adjust an oven rack to the middle position and heat the oven to 375 degrees.

2. Spread the tortilla chips over the rimmed baking sheet. Sprinkle half of the shredded cheese over the chips. Sprinkle the beans, olives, and jalapeño chiles evenly over the cheese. Sprinkle the remaining cheese over top.

3. Place the baking sheet in the oven and bake until the cheese is gooey and melted, 8 to 12 minutes.

4. Use oven mitts to transfer the baking sheet to a cooling rack (ask a grown-up for help). Dollop the mashed avocado evenly over top and sprinkle with the tomatoes. Drizzle with crema and sprinkle with cilantro. Use tongs to serve.

¿QUIÉN INVENTÓ LOS NACHOS? (WHO INVENTED NACHOS?)

Nachos were born in 1940, in Piedras Negras, a city in Coahuila, México, when a group of women from just-over-the-border in Texas walked into a restaurant and asked for a snack. Ignacio Anaya ran the restaurant, but didn't have any cooks at the moment, so he went into the kitchen and worked with the ingredients he could find: totopos (tortilla chips), Colby cheese, and pickled jalapeños. The women loved the crunchy, melty snack. Ignacio—Nacho for short—eventually moved to Eagle Pass, Texas, and opened a restaurant called Nacho's, where they served, no surprise, nachos! The simple original recipe remained a staple, but as nachos gained popularity (especially in the United States), they grew in layers and complexity. Suddenly, nachos included ground beef and guacamole, salsa, pico de gallo, sour cream, and more. In 1970, a Texas businessman brought nachos to the world with the addition of an emulsified nacho cheese sauce that didn't need to be refrigerated and was perfect for serving at sporting events.

TOSTADAS DE FRIJOLES Y QUESO
(BEAN AND CHEESE TOSTADAS)

A "tostada" can refer to a piece of toasted bread or to a corn tortilla that's fried or baked until crunchy and often loaded with toppings. The recipe here is from México, and it is basically an open-faced taco—a crispy shell topped with refried beans, queso fresco, crunchy lettuce, creamy avocado, and a good dollop of crema. Can you imagine a better combo than that?

You can also serve your tostadas with salsa or Pico de Gallo (page 172), if you want. If you can't find crema, you can use sour cream instead: For ½ cup sour cream, thin it with 2 tablespoons of water or 1 tablespoon of water and 1 tablespoon of lime juice.

 México

SERVES **6**

DIFFICULTY LEVEL

¡EN SUS MARCAS! Ready!

INGREDIENTS

- 1 (15-ounce) can **refried beans**
- ¼ cup **water**, plus extra as needed
- 6 store-bought **tostada shells**
- 1 cup crumbled **queso fresco** (4 ounces) or 1 cup shredded **mozzarella cheese** (4 ounces)
- 4 **romaine lettuce leaves**, thinly sliced
- 1 **large ripe avocado**, halved, pitted, and mashed with a fork (see page 57)

  Crema (or sour cream—see the note on the left)

  Hot sauce

¡LISTOS! Set!

EQUIPMENT

Small saucepan

Rubber spatula

Rimmed baking sheet

Oven mitts

Cooling rack

¡FUERA! Go!

1. Adjust an oven rack to the middle position and heat the oven to 350 degrees.

2. Put the refried beans and water into a small saucepan. Cook over medium-low heat, stirring constantly with a rubber spatula, until the beans are warm and have a spreadable consistency, about 5 minutes. (Add more water as needed, a tablespoon at a time, to loosen the beans.) Turn off the heat.

3. Place the tostada shells on a rimmed baking sheet. Divide the refried beans evenly between the tostada shells and spread into an even layer. Sprinkle the cheese evenly over top.

4. Place the baking sheet in the oven. Bake until the tostadas are warmed through, 3 to 5 minutes.

5. Use oven mitts to remove the baking sheet from the oven and transfer to a cooling rack (ask a grown-up for help). Top the tostadas with lettuce and avocado. Drizzle with crema and hot sauce to taste. Serve.

~~~~~~

TRANSFORMA LAS SOBRAS EN ALGO NUEVO (TURN LEFTOVERS INTO SOMETHING NEW)

I love to use leftovers in creative ways, so of course I love tostadas—they were invented as a way to use up leftover tortillas. Toasting or frying stale tortillas turns them crunchy and delicious. And then you can top them with other leftovers, if you want—genius!

SÁNDWICH TOSTADO "CARLITOS" DE JAMÓN, QUESO, Y TOMATE

(TOASTED HAM AND CHEESE SANDWICH WITH KETCHUP)

If you go to a cafe in Buenos Aires and order a coffee and a "tostado," you will receive a toasted sandwich composed of thin layers of bread with ham and cheese. It's made on white bread, has the crusts cut off, and can also be called a sandwich "de miga," which literally means "crumb." These white bread sandwiches are served all over Argentina, Uruguay, and Chile.

They're popular at parties, teas, birthdays, and more. They can be filled with ham and cheese, and sometimes other ingredients, from hard-boiled eggs and peppers to hearts of palm and olives to prosciutto and artichokes. There is a very special tostado in Argentina called "Carlitos," which is traditionally made with toasted white bread, ham, cheese, and . . . ketchup!

Argentina

SERVES **2**

DIFFICULTY LEVEL

INGREDIENTS

- 4 slices **hearty white sandwich bread**
- 3 tablespoons **ketchup**
- 4 slices **deli ham**
- 4 slices **deli mozzarella cheese**
- 1 tablespoon **olive oil**

¡LISTOS! **Set!**

EQUIPMENT

Cutting board

Butter knife

Chef's knife

Pastry brush

12-inch nonstick skillet with a lid

Spatula

Oven mitts

¡FUERA! **Go!**

1. Place the bread on a cutting board. Use a butter knife to spread the ketchup evenly over the bread. Divide the ham evenly between 2 slices of the bread, folding the ham as needed to fit the size of the bread. Top with the cheese.

2. Close the sandwiches and use a chef's knife to cut the crusts off on all four sides. (You might lose some of the ham, but I love to snack on those edges, so make sure to save them for later!)

3. Use a pastry brush to lightly brush the tops of both sandwiches with oil. Place both sandwiches in a 12-inch nonstick skillet, oiled side down. Lightly brush the second sides of the sandwiches with oil.

4. Cook the tostados over medium-low heat until golden brown, about 3 minutes. Use a spatula to flip the sandwiches (ask a grown-up for help).

5. Cover the skillet with the lid and cook until the second side is golden brown and the cheese is melted, 2 to 3 minutes. Turn off the heat.

6. Use oven mitts to remove the lid. Transfer the sandwiches to the cutting board. Let them cool slightly, about 1 minute. Cut each sandwich in half diagonally and serve.

❝ **'TWAS CHEESE-Y, HAM-Y, KETCHUP-Y, AND YUMMY!!!!! :)"**

—Claire, age 10

LA PIZZA RÁPIDA DE MI ABUELA
(MY ABUELA'S QUICK PIZZA)

When I was growing up, we rarely ordered pizza for takeout. But my abuela frequently made her "quick pizza." To me, this dish is as Argentinean as my childhood. She would use sliced white bread, toast it, and then pour some tomato sauce on top (hers was usually homemade). Then, she would add some mozzarella (or whatever cheese we had around), put it in the oven for a few minutes, and then sprinkle some oregano or red pepper flakes on top. And there you go! Pizza in less than 10 minutes. This is my version of my abuela's pizza rápida. I hope you like it!

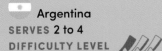 **Argentina**

SERVES **2 to 4**

DIFFICULTY LEVEL

¡EN SUS MARCAS!  Ready!

INGREDIENTS

- 4 slices **hearty white sandwich bread**, toasted
- ¼ cup canned **tomato sauce**
- 4 slices **deli mozzarella cheese**
- **Dried oregano** (optional)
- **Red pepper flakes** (optional)
- **Garlic powder** (optional)

¡LISTOS!  Set!

EQUIPMENT

- Rimmed baking sheet
- Parchment paper
- Spoon
- Oven mitts
- Cooling rack
- Spatula
- Cutting board
- Chef's knife

¡FUERA!  Go!

1. Adjust an oven rack to the middle position and heat the oven to 350 degrees. Line a rimmed baking sheet with parchment paper.

2. Place the toasted bread on the parchment-lined baking sheet. Use a spoon to divide the sauce evenly between the toast slices and spread into an even layer. Place 1 slice of cheese on each toast.

3. Place the baking sheet in the oven. Bake until the cheese is melted, 5 to 7 minutes.

4. Use oven mitts to transfer the baking sheet to a cooling rack (ask a grown-up for help). Use a spatula to transfer the pizzas to a cutting board. Sprinkle with oregano, pepper flakes, and/or garlic powder (if using). Cut each pizza into triangles and serve.

LOS INVENTOS DE MI ABUELA (MY ABUELA'S INVENTIONS)

I grew up with my abuela Porota, my mom's mom. She is the main reason why I cook. As a kid, I always thought she was a genius in the kitchen. I have so many memories of her inventing things for us to eat. She was the daughter of French immigrants—a first-generation Argentinean! She grew up listening to her elders tell stories of the old world of Europe and all the wonderful dishes they ate, so you can imagine her mind was always creating and in the clouds . . . just like mine! I always thought this pizza rápida was her invention, but little did I know that every abuela has a similar recipe at home.

AGUA FRESCA DE LIMÓN
(LIME WATER)

Aguas frescas are fresh fruit drinks that are very popular all over México. These refreshing beverages are typically served from large barrel-shaped containers called "vitroleros," in beautiful glasses, sometimes garnished with more fruit. You can also buy them from street vendors, and enjoy them alongside some tacos. One of my favorite varieties is lime, which in México is called limón. I use entire limes in this recipe so that you get the limiest possible flavor from both the juice and the peel.

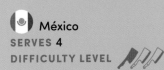 México

SERVES 4

DIFFICULTY LEVEL

¡EN SUS MARCAS!  Ready!

INGREDIENTS

- ¼ cup **sugar**
- 2 cups plus 2 cups **water**, measured separately
- 3 **limes**, cut in quarters, plus lime slices for serving

  Pinch **kosher salt**

  Ice

¡LISTOS! Set!

EQUIPMENT

Blender

Dish towel

Fine-mesh strainer

Pitcher

Large spoon

Serving glasses

¡FUERA!  Go!

1. Combine the sugar and 2 cups of water in a blender jar. Place the lid on top of the blender and hold the lid firmly in place with a folded dish towel. Turn on the blender and process until the sugar is completely dissolved, about 15 seconds. Stop the blender.

2. Add the lime quarters to the blender jar. Replace the lid and process for just 5 seconds—no more! Stop the blender.

3. Set a fine-mesh strainer over a pitcher. Pour the mixture from the blender through the strainer and discard the solids. Add the salt and the remaining 2 cups of water and stir with a large spoon until well combined.

4. Place the ice in serving glasses and pour the agua fresca over the ice. Add the lime slices and serve. (Agua fresca is best served immediately, but it can be refrigerated for up to 2 days.)

¿LIMA O LIMÓN? (LIME OR LEMON?)

Aguas frescas ("fresh waters") are made in many countries—and can be made from fruits, flowers, grains, or seeds, all mixed with water and sugar. They are an inexpensive way to make a delicious drink AND to use any leftover fruits, so nothing goes to waste. As a bonus, here is a little Spanish lesson related to this particular agua fresca: In México, "limón" means "lime." But in some other Spanish-speaking countries, "limón" means "lemon," and limes are called "limas." But guess what? In México, a lemon is called "limón amarillo," or "yellow lemon." Interesting, right?

AGUA FRESCA DE FRESA
(STRAWBERRY WATER)

There are many different types of agua fresca, but I think my favorite has to be agua fresca de fresa. Why? Because strawberries are my absolute favorite fruit. Fun fact: In México a strawberry is called "fresa," and in Argentina it's called a "frutilla." Spanish is fun!

 México

SERVES 6

DIFFICULTY LEVEL

INGREDIENTS

- 2 tablespoons **sugar**
- 3 cups plus 3 cups **water**, measured separately
- 3 cups **strawberries**, hulled and cut in half (see page 199)
- 2 tablespoons **lime juice**, squeezed from 1 lime (see page 20)
- Pinch **kosher salt**
- **Ice**

¡LISTOS! Set!

EQUIPMENT

- Blender
- Dish towel
- Fine-mesh strainer
- Pitcher
- Large spoon
- Serving glasses

¡FUERA! Go!

1. Combine the sugar and 3 cups of water in a blender jar. Place the lid on top of the blender and hold the lid firmly in place with a folded dish towel. Turn on the blender and process until the sugar is completely dissolved, about 15 seconds. Stop the blender.

2. Add the strawberries to the blender jar. Replace the lid and process for 10 to 15 seconds.

3. Set a fine-mesh strainer over a pitcher. Pour the mixture from the blender through the strainer, and use a large spoon to press on the solids to get as much liquid out as possible; discard the solids. Add the lime juice, salt, and the remaining 3 cups of water and stir until well combined.

4. Place the ice in serving glasses and pour the agua fresca over the ice. Serve. (Agua fresca is best served immediately, but it can be refrigerated for up to 2 days.)

AGUA FRESCA DE SANDÍA (WATERMELON WATER)

Agua Fresca de Sandía is one of my favorite ways to consume watermelon. The best watermelon will obviously make the best agua fresca. I love how refreshing it is—especially with a little bit of salt and lime juice.

To make Agua Fresca de Sandía: Use **3 cups** of **2-inch pieces of watermelon**, instead of the strawberries. Increase the lime juice to ½ cup (squeezed from 4 limes).

LICUADO DE BANANA
(BANANA SMOOTHIE)

Licuados are a fruit and milk beverage, the Latin American version of a smoothie. Made of different combinations of fruits and liquids, from water to fresh juice, they are many people's favorite bebida! Licuado de banana was one of the first recipes I ever made as a kid, and it is one of the most popular flavors in Argentina. I have vivid memories of preparing it, drinking it, and fighting with my brother for the last cup!

 Argentina

SERVES **2**

DIFFICULTY LEVEL

INGREDIENTS

2 **bananas**, peeled and broken into pieces

1 cup **milk**

1 cup **ice**

EQUIPMENT

Blender

Dish towel

Serving glasses

1. Put all the ingredients into a blender jar. Place the lid on top of the blender and hold the lid firmly in place with a folded dish towel. Turn on the blender and process until smooth, 1 to 2 minutes. Stop the blender.

2. Pour the licuado de banana into serving glasses and serve.

BEBE TUS FRUTAS (DRINK YOUR FRUITS)

For a long time, I grew up thinking that licuado de banana was an Argentinean invention! Turns out that it's made in many countries in Latin America, sometimes called a "batido". And it can be made with many fruits—not just bananas. Licuados are a great way to include fruits in your diet!

> **THE BANANA FLAVOR WAS SO GOOD AND YOU COULD ACTUALLY TASTE IT BECAUSE THE OTHER INGREDIENTS DIDN'T OVERPOWER THE FLAVOR. THIS SMOOTHIE WAS ALSO SUPER CREAMY BECAUSE OF THE MILK AND THE BANANA."**
>
> —Izzy, age 12

LICUADO TUTTI FRUTTI
(ALL-THE-FRUITS SMOOTHIE)

When I was growing up in Buenos Aires, nothing went to waste in my house. My mom made us eat everything! This licuado was a wonderful way to use up all the overripe fruit in our kitchen. Plus, it's delicious. Because its name means "todas las frutas" ("all the fruits"), you can reinvent it every time you make it, using whatever fruits you have on hand. Fruits I love to use include peaches, bananas, apples, pears, strawberries, blueberries, pineapple, oranges, and kiwis. This recipe is for a basic version with strawberries, orange, and pear, but feel free to experiment!

Argentina

SERVES 4

DIFFICULTY LEVEL

¡EN SUS MARCAS! Ready!

INGREDIENTS

1 cup **strawberries**, hulled and cut in half (see page 199)

1 **orange**, peeled and cut into 1-inch pieces (1 cup) (see page 198)

1 **pear**, peeled and cut into 1-inch pieces (1 cup) (see page 198)

2 cups **water**

1 cup **ice**

¡LISTOS! Set!

EQUIPMENT

Blender

Dish towel

Serving glasses

¡FUERA! Go!

1. Put all the ingredients into a blender jar. Place the lid on top of the blender and hold the lid firmly in place with a folded dish towel. Turn on the blender and process until smooth, 1 to 2 minutes. Stop the blender.

2. Pour the licuado tutti frutti into serving glasses and serve.

CHOCOLATE CALIENTE
(HOT CHOCOLATE)

Chocolate caliente, or hot chocolate, is consumed all over the world. Each country has its own particular way of preparing it. My abuela made chocolate caliente with "chocolate para taza," a bar of breakable chocolate sticks that came in a brightly colored pink package. I learned to make my favorite chocolate caliente in México, using a molinillo, a traditional wooden whisk—but you can replicate this using a wire whisk, no problem! Let me set your expectations: This is different from the typical American hot chocolate—it's not as sweet but is much more chocolaty. I like to use Taza brand Cacao Puro Mexican-style 70% Dark Chocolate Discs in this recipe.

 México

SERVES **4**

DIFFICULTY LEVEL

¡EN SUS MARCAS!  Ready!

INGREDIENTS

- 4 cups **milk**
- 5 ounces **Taza brand Cacao Puro Mexican-style 70% Dark Chocolate Discs**
- 2 **cinnamon sticks**

¡LISTOS! Set!

EQUIPMENT

Large saucepan

Wooden spoon

Whisk or molinillo

Serving mugs or cups

Spoon

¡FUERA! Go!

1. In a large saucepan, combine all the ingredients. Cook over medium-high heat, stirring constantly with a wooden spoon, until the chocolate melts, about 5 minutes. (Do not look away; the milk can boil very quickly!)

2. When the milk starts to foam up (but has not yet come to a boil), reduce the heat to medium-low. Simmer until the mixture has an even color, stirring often, about 5 minutes. Turn off the heat.

3. Let the mixture cool for 5 minutes. Remove the cinnamon sticks. Whisk vigorously to create a little bit of foam on the surface of the chocolate caliente (see the photo below). Serve in mugs, making sure to spoon some of the foam on top.

CÓMO HACER ESPUMA (HOW TO MAKE FOAM)

Whisk vigorously to create foam on the surface of the chocolate caliente.

EL SUBMARINO (THE SUBMARINE)

In Argentina, there is a chocolate caliente known as "el submarino," or "the submarine." You serve a glass of hot milk with a rectangle of chocolate on the side. You then proceed to drop the "submarine" (the chocolate!) into the milk and stir, stir, stir with a long silver spoon until it melts.

Cena
Dinner

ROPA VIEJA
(SHREDDED BEEF STEW)

Ropa vieja gets its name, which translates as "old clothes," in part because a pile of tender shredded beef and sliced onions and peppers *does* resemble a pile of clothes (learn more in "La historia de la ropa vieja" on page 124). Spanish colonizers first brought a version of the dish to the Caribbean back in the 1500s. Today, ropa vieja is made in many countries in Latin America, but it's by far the most popular in Cuba. Many families use flank steak in their ropa vieja, but I like to use chuck roast in my version because it has a little more fat and cooks up really tender. Make sure to ask your butcher to cut the chuck roast taller rather than wider—this will give you longer strands of beef when you shred the meat. And after you remove the pieces of carrot and celery in step 7, don't throw them out—eat them! I love to munch on them as a snack.

 Cuba

SERVES **8**

DIFFICULTY LEVEL

¡EN SUS MARCAS! Ready!

INGREDIENTS

1½ pounds **boneless beef chuck-eye roast**

2 teaspoons plus 1 teaspoon **kosher salt**, measured separately

½ teaspoon plus ⅛ teaspoon **pepper**, measured separately

1 tablespoon **olive oil**

1 **onion**, peeled and sliced thin (see page 19)

1 **green bell pepper**, stemmed, seeded, and sliced thin (see page 20)

3 **garlic cloves**, peeled and minced (see page 19)

2 teaspoons **dried oregano**

2 teaspoons **ground cumin**

2 teaspoons **paprika**

2 tablespoons **tomato paste**

¼ cup **white wine vinegar**

1 (14.5-ounce) can **crushed tomatoes**

1 cup **chicken broth**

2 large **celery ribs**, each cut into 2 pieces

1 large **carrot**, peeled and cut into 4 pieces

2 **bay leaves**

1 cup **pimento-stuffed green olives**, rinsed and sliced

¾ cup **jarred roasted red peppers**, sliced thin

⅓ cup chopped **fresh parsley** (see page 19)

¡LISTOS! Set!

EQUIPMENT

Paper towels

Dutch oven with a lid

Tongs

Large plate

Wooden spoon

Oven mitts

2 forks

¡FUERA! Go!

1. Pat the beef dry with paper towels. Sprinkle 2 teaspoons of salt and ½ teaspoon of pepper evenly over the beef.

2. In a Dutch oven, heat the oil over medium-high heat for about 1 minute (the oil should be hot but not smoking). Add the beef and cook until it is browned on the first side, 3 to 5 minutes. Use tongs to carefully flip the beef and cook until it is browned on the second side, 3 to 5 minutes. Transfer the beef to a plate and set it aside. (Do not discard the drippings left in the pot—they will be key to the flavor!)

3. Add the onion, bell pepper, remaining 1 teaspoon of salt, and remaining ⅛ teaspoon of pepper to the now-empty pot. Cook, stirring occasionally with a wooden spoon, until the vegetables are softened and just beginning to brown, 5 to 7 minutes.

KEEP GOING

❝ IT HAD A LOT OF FLAVOR. THE GREEN OLIVES SOUNDED WEIRD, BUT AFTER TASTING THEM IN THE STEW, THEY MADE SENSE BECAUSE OF THE TEXTURE AND SALTINESS. THEY WERE A SURPRISE.”

—Sebastian, age 12

4. Stir in the garlic, oregano, cumin, and paprika and cook for 30 seconds. Stir in the tomato paste and cook for 1 minute. Stir in the vinegar and cook, scraping up all the browned bits on the bottom of the pot, until the liquid evaporates, about 1 minute.

5. Add the tomatoes and broth, bring to a simmer, and cook for 5 minutes. Return the beef and any accumulated juices to the pot. Add the celery, carrot, and bay leaves and bring to a boil.

6. Reduce the heat to low; cover the pot with a lid; and cook until the meat is fork-tender and falls apart easily, 2½ to 3 hours. Turn off the heat.

7. Use oven mitts to remove the lid. Use tongs to remove the celery, carrot, and bay leaves. (Save the celery and carrot for a snack!)

8. Transfer the beef to a clean large plate and let it cool slightly. Use 2 forks to shred the beef (see the photo below left).

9. Return the shredded beef to the pot, add the olives and red peppers (save a few to garnish each serving), and stir to combine. Heat the ropa vieja over medium heat until it's warmed through, about 5 minutes. Turn off the heat. Season with salt and pepper to taste. Sprinkle the parsley over the top. Serve, sprinkling each portion with remaining red peppers.

CÓMO DESMENUZAR LA CARNE DE RES (HOW TO SHRED THE BEEF)

Use 2 forks to shred the beef into pieces.

LA HISTORIA DE LA ROPA VIEJA (THE STORY OF ROPA VIEJA)

The name "ropa vieja" ("old clothes") has another, more magical origin story: Legend has it that, once upon a time, a very poor man shredded his own clothes and put them into a pot to cook because he could not afford to buy food for his family. He prayed over the pot, and a miracle happened—the pot of shredded old clothes transformed into a pot of meat stew!

GUISO DE LENTEJAS
(LENTIL STEW)

When I was growing up, we had guiso de lentejas all the time during the winter months—it's a warm, filling stew that's the perfect thing to eat when it's chilly outside. When I started living on my own, it was one of my favorite recipes to make because it reminded me of home. Today, I make it every winter to feed my friends. You can make this guiso vegetarian (omit the kielbasa and use vegetable broth), or you can make it with other cuts of meat, such as chorizo, cubed beef, or bacon. It always saves the day! Potatoes can be difficult to prep—because they're starchy, they can easily stick to your knife. Be sure to ask a grown-up to help you cut them. It's important to soak your lentils for 1 hour before you start the recipe—this helps them cook faster. Serve your guiso de lentejas with some fresh crusty bread.

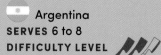 **Argentina**

SERVES 6 to 8

DIFFICULTY LEVEL

¡EN SUS MARCAS! Ready!

●●●●●●●●●●●●●●●●●●

INGREDIENTS

- 1 cup **dried brown lentils**, soaked in water for 1 hour and drained
- 1 tablespoon plus 1 tablespoon **olive oil**, measured separately
- 8 ounces **kielbasa sausage**, sliced into ¼-inch-thick half-moons
- 1 **onion**, peeled and chopped fine (see page 19)
- 1 **red bell pepper**, stemmed, seeded, and chopped fine (see page 20)
- 1 tablespoon **dried oregano**
- 3 **garlic cloves**, peeled and minced (see page 19)
- 1 teaspoon **dried thyme**
- 2 tablespoons **tomato paste**
- 5 cups **chicken broth**
- 2 **small russet potatoes**, peeled and cut into 1-inch pieces
- 2 **small sweet potatoes**, peeled and cut into 1-inch pieces
- 1 **bay leaf**
- 1 teaspoon **kosher salt**
- ½ teaspoon **pepper**
- Pinch **red pepper flakes** (optional)

¡LISTOS! Set!

●●●●●●●●●●●●●●●●●

EQUIPMENT

Dutch oven with a lid	Plate
Wooden spoon	Oven mitts
Slotted spoon	

¡FUERA! Go!

●●●●●●●●●●●●●●●●●●

1. In a Dutch oven, heat 1 tablespoon of oil over medium-high heat for about 1 minute (the oil should be hot but not smoking). Add the kielbasa and cook, stirring often with a wooden spoon, until the edges start to brown, 2 to 4 minutes.

2. Use a slotted spoon to transfer the kielbasa to a plate.

3. Add the remaining 1 tablespoon of oil to the now-empty pot along with the onion and bell pepper. Cook, stirring occasionally, until the vegetables start to brown, 3 to 5 minutes.

4. Add the oregano, garlic, and thyme and cook for 30 seconds. Stir in the tomato paste and cook for 1 minute. Add the drained lentils and stir until well combined. Add the broth, russet potatoes, sweet potatoes, bay leaf, salt, pepper, and cooked kielbasa and stir, scraping up all the browned bits on the bottom of the pot.

5. Bring the mixture to a boil. Reduce the heat to medium-low, cover the pot with a lid, and cook for 30 minutes.

6. Use oven mitts to remove the lid. Continue to cook until the lentils are tender, 5 to 10 minutes. Turn off the heat.

7. Season with salt and pepper to taste. Stir in the pepper flakes (if you like your stew a little spicy!). Serve.

TODO SOBRE LAS LENTEJAS (ALL ABOUT LENTILS)

Lentils are legumes—they're related to peas and beans, such as chickpeas and pinto beans. At the store, you'll see a colorful variety of lentils: the wide, flat brown lentils used in this recipe; shiny black (or beluga) lentils; olive-colored French green lentils; and red lentils, which are actually just brown or green lentils that have had their skins removed and been split in two!

PASTEL DE PAPAS

(BEEF SHEPHERD'S PIE)

 **Argentina**

SERVES **8**

DIFFICULTY LEVEL

¡EN SUS MARCAS! Ready!

●●●·●·●●●●●●·●●●●●

INGREDIENTS

- 1 recipe **Picadillo** (page 130)
- 2 tablespoons **olive oil**
- 3 pounds **russet potatoes**, peeled and cut into 1-inch pieces
- 1 tablespoon plus ½ teaspoon **kosher salt**, measured separately
- 8 tablespoons **unsalted butter**
- 1 cup **milk**
- 1 tablespoon **sugar** (optional)

¡LISTOS! Set!

●●●●●●●·●●·●●●●●●●●●

EQUIPMENT

13-by-9-inch baking dish

Dutch oven

Ruler

Paring knife

Colander

Potato masher

Rubber spatula

Fork

Oven mitts

Cooling rack

When I was growing up, my abuela would make us a HUGE pastel de papas. She used a fork to draw lines in the mashed-potato topping, so she knew which section had no olives and which had olives but no raisins. (This was to please my picky cousins and brother—I would eat everything, and I pretty much still do!) She also always sprinkled a tiny bit of sugar on top of the potatoes before they baked so that they would get even more brown and delicious in the oven. Potatoes can be difficult to prep—because they're starchy, they can easily stick to your knife. Be sure to ask a grown-up to help you cut them. Make the Picadillo before you start this recipe.

1. Adjust an oven rack to the middle position and heat the oven to 400 degrees. Add the oil to a 13-by-9-inch baking dish and use your hands to rub it all over the dish and grease it evenly.

2. Put the potatoes in a Dutch oven. Add water to cover the potatoes by 1 inch. Add 1 tablespoon of salt. Bring to a boil over medium-high heat. Cook until the potatoes are tender and cooked through, 10 to 15 minutes (you can check for doneness by piercing the potatoes with the tip of a paring knife—the knife should slide easily in and out of the potatoes; ask a grown-up for help).

3. Place a colander in the sink. Ask a grown-up to drain the potatoes. Transfer the potatoes back to the pot. Add the butter, milk, and remaining ½ teaspoon of salt and use a potato masher to mash the potatoes until there are no visible pieces remaining.

4. Add one-third of the mashed potatoes to the greased dish and spread them into an even layer with a rubber spatula. Add the picadillo (this can be cold or hot) and spread it into an even layer. Dollop the remaining mashed potatoes over the picadillo and spread them into an even layer.

5. Use a fork to add texture to the top layer of potatoes following the photo below. Sprinkle the sugar (if using) evenly over the potatoes.

6. Place the baking dish in the oven. Bake until the pastel de papas is bubbling around the edges and browned on top, about 30 minutes. (If you want more browning, you can turn on the broiler and broil until the top is well browned, about 2 minutes.)

7. Use oven mitts to transfer the baking dish to a cooling rack (ask a grown-up for help). Let the pastel de papas cool for 15 minutes. Serve.

~~~~~~~~~~~~~~~~~~~~~~~~~

EL MISMO PLATO CON DIFERENTES NOMBRES (SAME DISH, DIFFERENT NAMES)

Baked dishes of saucy cooked meat topped with mashed potatoes appear on dinner tables in many different countries—and go by many different names. In countries such as Argentina, Chile, and Uruguay, it's called "pastel de papas" ("potato pie") or "pastel de carne" ("meat pie"). In the United Kingdom, it's called "shepherd's pie" if the filling is made with lamb or mutton and "cottage pie" if it's made with beef. In France, it's called "hachis Parmentier" and layers leftover beef stew with mashed potatoes and cheese. (The name comes from the pharmacist Antoine-Augustin Parmentier, who advocated for the nutritional value of the potato.)

CÓMO CREAR TEXTURA (HOW TO CREATE TEXTURE)

I like to use a fork to make lines across the mashed potatoes. It adds some texture, and is exactly what my abuela did when making this dish. Just drag the end of the fork across the potatoes to create textured lines.

PICADILLO
(GROUND BEEF HASH)

Picadillo—spiced ground meat cooked with a wide variety of other ingredients—is popular across Latin America. Some picadillos include fruit, some have potatoes, some are spicy, but all have ground meat! You can eat your picadillo lots of different ways: alongside rice, plantains, or mashed potatoes; as a filling for empanadas or tacos; or even as a base for pastelón or Pastel de Papas (page 128). A few years ago, when I was selling empanadas de picadillo, some customers told me that my empanadas were salty. I didn't understand why, until I realized that I hadn't rinsed the olives. You must rinse the olives!

 **Argentina**

SERVES **8**

DIFFICULTY LEVEL

¡EN SUS MARCAS! Ready!

●●●●●●●●●●●●●●●●●●

INGREDIENTS

- 1 tablespoon **olive oil**
- 2 pounds **80 percent lean ground beef**
- 2 teaspoons **kosher salt**
- ½ teaspoon **pepper**
- 2 **onions**, peeled and chopped fine (see page 19)
- 2 **red bell peppers**, stemmed, seeded, and chopped fine (see page 20)
- 3 tablespoons **ground cumin**
- 2 tablespoons **paprika**
- 1 tablespoon **dried oregano**
- 2 teaspoons **sugar**
- ⅛ teaspoon **red pepper flakes**
- 1 cup **water**, **beef broth**, or **chicken broth**
- 1 cup **pitted green olives** (picholine or Spanish), rinsed and sliced
- ½ cup **raisins**

¡LISTOS! Set!

●●●●●●●●●●●●●●●●●●

EQUIPMENT

Dutch oven

Wooden spoon

Slotted spoon

Medium bowl

¡FUERA! Go!

●●●●●●●●●●●●●●●●●●●●

1. In a Dutch oven, heat the oil over medium-high heat for about 1 minute (the oil should be hot but not smoking). Add the ground beef, salt, and pepper and cook, breaking up the meat with a wooden spoon, until the beef is evenly browned, 10 to 12 minutes. Turn off the heat.

2. Use a slotted spoon to transfer the beef to a medium bowl.

3. Return the pot to medium-high heat and add the onions and bell peppers. Cook, stirring occasionally, until the vegetables are softened, about 5 minutes.

4. Stir in the cumin, paprika, oregano, sugar, and pepper flakes and cook for 1 minute. Stir in the cooked beef and any accumulated juices along with the water, scraping up all the browned bits on the bottom of the pot.

5. Bring the mixture to a boil and let it boil rapidly for 2 minutes. Reduce the heat to medium-low and cook, stirring occasionally, until the mixture is fragrant and the meat is dark brown, about 10 minutes. Turn off the heat.

6. Stir in the olives and raisins. Serve. (The picadillo can be refrigerated for up to 4 days or frozen for up to 2 weeks.)

PICADILLO POPULAR (POPULAR PICADILLO)

Picadillo is popular from the Caribbean all the way through South America in places such as Puerto Rico, Cuba, the República Dominicana, México, Costa Rica, Colombia, Brasil, and Argentina. Its name comes from the word "picar" ("to mince"), which makes sense given that all picadillo recipes include ground ("minced") meat. The exact combination of spices and the rest of the picadillo ingredients vary from country to country and even from family to family within the same country! Picadillo recipes might include vegetables, such as tomatoes, potatoes, peppers, onions, and peas, plus briny capers and olives and sometimes sweet raisins.

ENTRAÑA AL HORNO CON CHIMICHURRI

(OVEN-BAKED SKIRT STEAK WITH CHIMICHURRI SAUCE)

Argentina
SERVES 4
DIFFICULTY LEVEL

¡EN SUS MARCAS! Ready!

INGREDIENTS

1 recipe **Chimichurri** (page 174)

1½ pounds **skirt steak**

1 teaspoon **kosher salt**

1 tablespoon **olive oil**

¡LISTOS! Set!

EQUIPMENT

2 cooling racks

Rimmed baking sheet

Paper towels

Oven mitts

Tongs

Instant-read thermometer

Cutting board

Chef's knife

Serving platter

Skirt steak, which is called "entraña" in Argentina, is an inexpensive cut of meat that's prized for its flavor. It's typically grilled, but as long as you cook entraña quickly at a high temperature (I use the oven in this recipe), it will turn out great—browned on the outside and medium-rare on the inside. Plus, you will have dinner in just about 30 minutes! I love to serve this with garlicky Chimichurri and an Ensalada Mixta (page 176).

¡FUERA! Go!

●●●●●●●●●●●●●●●●●●●●

1. Adjust an oven rack to the middle position and heat the oven to 400 degrees. Set a cooling rack in a rimmed baking sheet.

2. Pat the steak dry with paper towels. Sprinkle the salt evenly over both sides of the steak. Place the steak on the rack set in the baking sheet. Drizzle the oil over both sides of the steak. Wash your hands.

3. Place the baking sheet in the oven and roast for 5 minutes. Use oven mitts to transfer the baking sheet to a second cooling rack (ask a grown-up for help).

4. Use tongs to flip the steak. Return the baking sheet to the oven and roast for 5 more minutes.

5. Turn on the broiler. Broil the steak until it's browned on top and registers 125 degrees (for medium-rare) on an instant-read thermometer inserted into the thickest part of the steak, 2 to 5 minutes.

6. Use oven mitts to transfer the baking sheet to the cooling rack (ask a grown-up for help). Let the steak rest for 10 minutes. Transfer the steak to a cutting board. Use a chef's knife to slice the steak across the grain (see the photo on the right).

7. Transfer the steak to a serving platter. Serve, passing the chimichurri separately.

CÓMO CORTAR LA ENTRAÑA (HOW TO SLICE SKIRT STEAK) 〜〜〜〜〜

Use a chef's knife to slice the steak across the grain.

CAUSA DE ATÚN
(COLD TUNA AND POTATO CASSEROLE)

Causa de atún, chilled layers of mashed potatoes and tuna flavored with tangy lime juice and spicy ají amarillo chile paste, is a classic Peruvian dish. In Perú, it is typically served as a small appetizer made of two layers of potato surrounding one layer of tuna. In restaurants, you will see each serving elaborately garnished with tomatoes, olives, fresh herbs, avocado, or hard-boiled eggs. One of my first roommates in Jersey City was from Perú, and she introduced me to causa de atún, which she

would make every Christmas alongside a chicken cooked in Coca-Cola (really!). I like to make this homier version that you can bring to the table and serve family-style. Potatoes can be difficult to prep—because they're starchy, they can easily stick to your knife. Be sure to ask a grown-up to help you cut them. Look for bright-yellow ají amarillo paste in the Latin section of your grocery store, in Latin markets, or online.

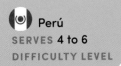 Perú

SERVES **4 to 6**

DIFFICULTY LEVEL

¡EN SUS MARCAS! Ready!

INGREDIENTS

POTATOES

1 pound **Yukon Gold potatoes**, peeled and cut into 1-inch pieces

1 tablespoon plus ½ teaspoon **kosher salt**, measured separately

¼ cup **olive oil**, plus extra for serving dish

1-2 tablespoons **ají amarillo chile paste**

¼ teaspoon **pepper**

¼ cup **lime juice**, squeezed from 2 limes (see page 20)

TUNA

3 (5-ounce) cans **solid white tuna in water**, drained and flaked

¼ cup finely chopped **red onion** (see page 19)

3 tablespoons **mayonnaise**

1 tablespoon **lime juice**, squeezed from ½ lime (see page 20)

1 tablespoon minced **fresh parsley** (see page 19)

OPTIONAL GARNISHES

1 **avocado**, halved, pitted, and sliced (see page 57)

2 **Huevos Duros**, peeled and finely chopped (see page 87)

3 tablespoons **pitted black olives**, rinsed and finely chopped

¡LISTOS! Set!

EQUIPMENT

Large saucepan

Ruler

Paring knife

Colander

Potato ricer or potato masher

2 medium bowls

Fork

Plastic wrap

Rubber spatula

Small, deep serving dish (about 1 quart, preferably glass)

¡FUERA! Go!

1. For the potatoes: Put the potatoes in a large saucepan. Add water to cover the potatoes by 1 inch. Add 1 tablespoon of salt. Bring to a boil over medium-high heat. Cook until the potatoes are tender and cooked through, 10 to 15 minutes (you can check for doneness by piercing the potatoes with the tip of a paring knife—the knife should slide easily in and out of the potatoes; ask a grown-up for help).

2. Place a colander in the sink. Ask a grown-up to drain the potatoes. Pass the potatoes through a potato ricer set over a medium bowl. (If you don't have a potato ricer, you can mash them with a potato masher until no visible potato chunks remain.) Let the potatoes cool for about 15 minutes.

KEEP GOING

> I LIKE HOW THE POTATOES AND TUNA COMPLEMENTED EACH OTHER WITH THE SMALL SPICE IN THE POTATOES."

—Zoe, age 13

3. For the tuna: While the potatoes cool, in a second medium bowl, combine all the tuna ingredients. Use a fork to stir until the mixture is well combined. Season with salt and pepper to taste. Cover the bowl with plastic wrap and refrigerate it until you're ready to use it.

4. Once the potatoes are cool, use a rubber spatula to stir in the oil, ají amarillo, pepper, ¼ cup lime juice, and remaining ½ teaspoon salt.

5. Drizzle a little bit of oil in the bottom of the serving dish and use your hands to rub it all over the dish. Add one-third of the mashed potatoes to the serving dish and spread them into an even layer. Add half of the tuna mixture and spread it into an even layer on top of the potatoes. Continue layering with half the remaining mashed potatoes, then the remaining tuna mixture, and finally the remaining mashed potatoes, spreading each addition into an even layer.

6. Cover the dish with plastic wrap and refrigerate it for at least 30 minutes or up to 24 hours before serving. Serve with avocado, Huevos Duros, and/or black olives, if using.

AJÍ AMARILLO: PICANTE Y COLORIDO (AJÍ AMARILLO: SPICY AND COLORFUL)

Bright yellow-orange ají amarillo chiles are one of the most important ingredients in Peruvian cooking. These chiles are definitely on the spicy side, but they also have a unique fruity flavor. To make ají amarillo paste—used in lots of Peruvian recipes—the fresh chiles are quickly boiled and then pureed until they have a smooth texture. In major American grocery stores you might see it labeled as "yellow hot pepper paste."

ARROZ CON POLLO
(RICE WITH CHICKEN)

Arroz con pollo (literally "rice with chicken") came to Latin America from Spain hundreds of years ago. Just about every country in Latin America has their own version of arroz con pollo, and even in a single country, each family has their own particular recipe. What do they all have in common? Well-seasoned rice cooked with a sofrito (see "Todo sobre el sofrito" on page 141) and juicy chicken—it's a whole meal in one pot! I learned to make arroz con pollo from my mom—

and there isn't really any reason to call this version Argentinean other than the fact that both my mom and I are from there! You can substitute paella seasoning for the saffron, but read the instructions for the amount to use per cup of liquid. To quickly thaw the peas, place them in a heatproof bowl and cover them with boiling water. Let the peas sit for 3 minutes to warm through, and then drain them in a colander in the sink.

🇦🇷 Argentina

SERVES 6

DIFFICULTY LEVEL

¡EN SUS MARCAS! Ready!

INGREDIENTS

- 2 cups **water**
- Pinch to ¼ teaspoon **saffron threads**
- 1 **large onion**, peeled and chopped (see page 19)
- 1 **red bell pepper**, stemmed, seeded, and chopped (see page 20)
- 3 **garlic cloves**, peeled (see page 19)
- 6 (5- to 7-ounce) **bone-in chicken thighs**
- ½ teaspoon **pepper**
- 1 tablespoon plus ½ teaspoon **kosher salt**, measured separately
- 1 tablespoon **olive oil**
- 1 tablespoon **dried oregano**
- 1 tablespoon **paprika**
- 2 tablespoons **red wine vinegar**
- 2 cups **long-grain white rice**
- 2 cups **chicken broth**
- 2 cups **frozen peas**, thawed (see the note on the left)
- ¼ cup chopped **fresh parsley** (see page 19)

¡LISTOS! Set!

EQUIPMENT

Small bowl	Tongs
Food processor	Plate
Paper towels	Wooden spoon
Dutch oven with a lid	Oven mitts

¡FUERA! Go!

1. Combine the water and saffron in a small bowl and set it aside (the saffron will bloom in the water and release its flavor and color).

2. Add the onion, bell pepper, and garlic to a food processor. Lock the lid into place. Hold down the pulse button for 1 second and then release it. Repeat until the vegetables are finely chopped, about ten 1-second pulses. (Don't process the vegetables or they will turn into a puree!) Remove the lid and carefully remove the processor blade (ask a grown-up for help). Set the vegetables aside.

3. Pat the chicken dry with paper towels. Sprinkle the chicken evenly with the pepper and 1 tablespoon of salt. Wash your hands.

4. In a Dutch oven, heat the oil over medium-high heat for about 1 minute (the oil should be hot but not smoking). Use tongs to place 3 pieces of chicken skin side down in the pot. Cook until the chicken is browned on the first side, about 5 minutes.

5. Use clean tongs to flip the chicken and cook until it is browned on the second side, about 5 minutes. Transfer the chicken to a plate (don't forget to use clean tongs!). Repeat cooking with the remaining 3 pieces of chicken and transfer to plate.

6. Add the chopped onion, bell pepper, and garlic (your sofrito!) and the remaining ½ teaspoon of salt to the now-empty pot. Cook, stirring often with a wooden spoon, until the vegetables are fragrant and softened, 3 to 5 minutes (if the bottom of your pot starts browning too quickly, reduce the heat to medium).

KEEP GOING

7. Stir in the oregano and paprika and cook for 30 seconds. Add the vinegar and cook, scraping up all the browned bits on the bottom of the pot, until the liquid has evaporated, about 1 minute.

8. Reduce the heat to medium; add the rice; and stir until the rice is well coated with the sofrito and spices, about 1 minute. Add the saffron water and broth.

9. Nestle the chicken in the rice. Increase the heat to high and bring the mixture to a boil. Reduce the heat to medium-low and cook until the liquid starts to reduce, 10 to 12 minutes (the liquid should be simmering at this point—small bubbles should break often across the surface of the mixture).

10. Reduce the heat to low and cover the pot with a lid, making sure that it has a good seal (if not, ask a grown-up to help you wrap the lid with aluminum foil to stop the steam from escaping). Cook for 20 minutes. Turn off the heat and let it sit for 7 minutes (no peeking!).

11. Use oven mitts to remove the lid and add the peas. (There may be a little bit of liquid remaining at the bottom of the pot—this is OK. I do not like a dry arroz con pollo!) Let the arroz con pollo sit uncovered for 10 more minutes. Serve, sprinkling individual portions with parsley.

IT WAS AN EXCELLENT DISH. FULL OF COLORS. THE RICE WAS DELICIOUS AND THE CHICKEN TENDER."

—Markos, age 9

TODO SOBRE EL SOFRITO

(ALL ABOUT SOFRITO)

At its simplest, sofrito is a sautéed mix of aromatic vegetables, such as onions, garlic, chiles, tomatoes, and cilantro, that forms the flavor base for dishes across Latin America. (The word "sofrito" roughly translates as "lightly fried.") Different countries use different ingredients in their sofritos, and the ingredients can vary even from dish to dish, lending them slightly different flavors and vastly different colors, from green to red to orange. In Portugal and Brasil, they call it "refogado"; in France, "mirepoix"; in Germany, "Suppengrün"; in Italy, "soffritto"; and in Cajun cooking (from the southern United States), the "Holy Trinity."

MOQUECA DE CAMARÓN
(SHRIMP STEW)

I tried moqueca de camarón, a coconutty shrimp stew from Brasil, for the first time many years ago at a hair salon in Newark, New Jersey. Yes, you read that right—a hair salon! I used to get my hair cut by a Brazilian hairstylist who was so popular that her salon was always superbusy, and every time I went, I ended up spending hours there. But all of her customers were friendly—so friendly that many of them brought food to the salon to share. And that's how I tried my first of many moquecas! Here is my humble version. Serve it with Arroz Blanco (page 154).

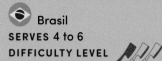 Brasil
SERVES 4 to 6
DIFFICULTY LEVEL

¡EN SUS MARCAS! Ready!
●●·●●●●●●●●··●●●●

INGREDIENTS

- 2 tablespoons **olive oil**
- 1 **red onion**, peeled and chopped fine (see page 19)
- 1 **green bell pepper**, stemmed, seeded, and cut into ½-inch pieces (see page 20)
- 2 **garlic cloves**, peeled and minced (see page 19)
- 1 teaspoon **kosher salt**
- 3 **plum tomatoes**, cored and chopped into ½-inch pieces (about 1 cup) (see page 67)
- ½ cup canned **coconut milk**
- ¼ cup minced **fresh cilantro** (see page 19)
- 1 pound **frozen peeled and deveined large shrimp** (26 to 30 per pound), thawed
- 2 **limes**, cut into wedges

¡LISTOS! Set!

EQUIPMENT

Dutch oven

Wooden spoon

¡FUERA! Go!
●●●·●●·●●●·●●●·●●●

1. In a Dutch oven, heat the oil over medium heat for about 1 minute (the oil should be hot but not smoking). Add the onion, bell peppers, garlic, and salt and cook, stirring occasionally with a wooden spoon, until the vegetables are softened, about 5 minutes.

2. Add the tomatoes, coconut milk, and half of the cilantro and stir until the mixture is well combined. Add the shrimp and cook until it turns pink, 5 to 7 minutes. Turn off the heat.

3. Season with salt to taste. Sprinkle the remaining cilantro over top and serve with the lime wedges.

~~~~~~~~~~~~~~~~~~~~~~~~

EL GUISO DE MARISCOS MÁS AMADO DE BRASIL (BRAZIL'S BELOVED SEAFOOD STEW)

Moqueca is one of Brasil's most beloved dishes—it's a stew featuring fish and/or shellfish traditionally cooked in a clay pot along with onions, tomatoes, peppers, and cilantro. There are different versions of moqueca made in different states along Brasil's long coastline. Moqueca baiana, from the northeastern state of Bahia, includes coconut milk and is traditionally served with dendê (red palm) oil and a hot sauce made from malagueta chiles. Moqueca capixaba, from the southeastern state of Espírito Santo, skips the coconut milk and is served with olive oil and annatto oil, made from bright-red achiote (annatto seeds). And moqueca paraense, from the northern state of Pará, includes yuca starch and juice (see "¿Qué es la yuca?" on page 164) along with jambu, a leafy herb.

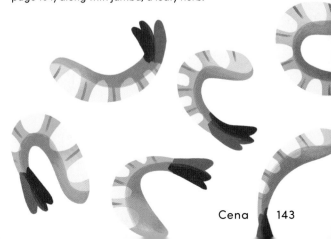

GAZPACHO (CHILLED TOMATO SOUP)

Argentina
SERVES 4 to 6 (Makes 6 cups)
DIFFICULTY LEVEL

¡EN SUS MARCAS! Ready!

INGREDIENTS

- 1 pound (about 6 **small**) **plum tomatoes**, cored, halved, seeded, and chopped (see page 67)
- 1 **cucumber**, peeled, halved lengthwise (the long way), seeded, and chopped
- 1 **red bell pepper**, stemmed, seeded, and chopped (see page 20)
- 1 slice **hearty white sandwich bread**, the crust removed
- 1 cup cold **water**
- ¼ cup **red wine vinegar**
- 3 tablespoons **olive oil**, plus extra for serving
- 3 **garlic cloves**, peeled (see page 19)
- 2 teaspoons **kosher salt**
- **Hot sauce** (optional)

¡LISTOS! Set!

EQUIPMENT

Blender

Dish towel

Large glass pitcher

Rubber spatula

Serving glasses

When I was growing up, my mom would make us gazpacho during the summer months, when there are always plenty of beautiful, ripe tomatoes. Since gazpacho is a cold soup, it's perfect to eat when it's hot outside. My mom's version is similar to gazpacho andaluz, which hails from southern Spain and gets its creamy texture from a secret ingredient: bread! I make my gazpacho in the blender, which gives you a very smooth soup—and also means that you do not need to peel the tomatoes, which is a bonus!

¡FUERA! Go!

1. Place half of all the ingredients (except the hot sauce) in the blender jar. Place the lid on top and hold the lid firmly in place with a folded dish towel. Turn on the blender and process until the mixture is smooth, about 1 minute. Stop the blender.

2. Transfer the mixture to a large glass pitcher. Repeat processing with the remaining ingredients and transfer them to the pitcher. Use a rubber spatula to stir until the gazpacho is well combined. Season with salt and pepper to taste.

3. Place the pitcher in the refrigerator for at least 30 minutes to chill. While the gazpacho chills, place the serving glasses in the freezer to chill.

4. Serve the gazpacho in the chilled glasses and drizzle with hot sauce (if using) and extra olive oil. (The gazpacho can be refrigerated in an airtight container for up to 2 days.)

UNA SOPA, DOS CONTINENTES (ONE SOUP, TWO CONTINENTS)

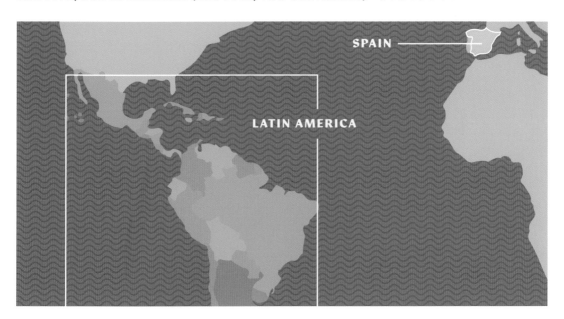

The earliest recipes for gazpacho didn't contain any tomatoes. Instead they were made with ingredients such as almonds, bread, olive oil, garlic, and vinegar. (Tomatoes arrived in Spain only after the conquistadores brought them back from the Americas.) Today, you'll find many different versions of this famous chilled soup in Spain as well as throughout Latin America. Some are made with bread, some without, and others, such as ajo blanco, are still tomato-free (ajo blanco is made with almonds, bread, and garlic). In español, we have a saying, "de gazpacho no hay empacho," which loosely translates as "you're never too full to eat more gazpacho"—but is really a way of saying "you can't get too much of a good thing."

TOMATES RELLENOS
(STUFFED TOMATOES)

 **Argentina**

SERVES **6**

DIFFICULTY LEVEL

¡EN SUS MARCAS! Ready!

INGREDIENTS

2 cups cooked **white rice**, cooled (or left over) (see Arroz Blanco, page 154)

6 **beefsteak tomatoes** (6 to 8 ounces each)

½ cup **frozen peas**, thawed (see the note on the left)

6 slices **deli ham**, chopped into ½-inch pieces

1 cup **mayonnaise**

1 tablespoon **olive oil**

1 teaspoon **cider vinegar**

3 tablespoons plus 1 tablespoon minced **fresh parsley**, measured separately

Tomates rellenos are another recipe that celebrates peak tomato season. These stuffed tomatoes look fancy, so you'll often see them on the table during the holidays in Argentina, but they're very easy to make. One of the best parts? You can swap out some of the ingredients to use whatever you have on hand or whatever you like best (see "Prepara tu relleno favorito" on the far right). Look for plump, firm tomatoes that are a little bit flat on the bottom—this will help them sit up straight on the serving platter! If your tomatoes are more rounded, you can remove a very thin slice from the bottom of each tomato to give it a flat base. To quickly thaw the peas, place them in a heatproof bowl and cover them with boiling water. Let the peas sit for 3 minutes to warm through, and then drain them in a colander in the sink.

¡LISTOS! Set!

EQUIPMENT

Cutting board

Chef's knife

Spoon

Rimmed baking sheet

Medium bowl

Serving platter

1. Place the tomatoes on a cutting board. Slice off the tops and then core, seed, and hollow out the tomatoes following the photos on the right.

2. Sprinkle a pinch of salt inside each tomato. Place the tomatoes cut side down on a rimmed baking sheet to drain.

3. In a medium bowl, use a spoon to combine the rice, peas, and ham, breaking up any clumps of rice. Add the mayonnaise, oil, vinegar, and 3 tablespoons of parsley and stir gently until the mixture is well combined and the ham is evenly distributed. Season with salt and pepper to taste.

4. Transfer the tomatoes, cut side up, to a serving platter. Divide the rice mixture evenly among the tomatoes. Sprinkle the remaining 1 tablespoon of parsley over top. Refrigerate the tomatoes for 20 minutes before serving.

COMO PREPARAR LOS TOMATES (HOW TO PREPARE TOMATOES)

1. Use a chef's knife to slice off the top of each tomato (like a lid).

2. Use a spoon to scoop out the core, seeds, and pulp of each tomato, creating a hollow tomato (kind of like hollowing out a pumpkin).

HEMISFERIOS OPUESTOS, ESTACIONES OPUESTAS (OPPOSITE HEMISPHERES, OPPOSITE SEASONS)

Geographically, most of Latin America lies in the southern hemisphere, below the equator. At any given moment, the season in the southern hemisphere is always the opposite of whatever it is in the northern hemisphere. When it is winter in Canada, it is summer in Argentina. When it is spring in Uruguay, it is fall in the United States. These opposite seasons occur because the Earth is tilted at an angle as it travels in its orbit around the Sun. When a hemisphere is angled toward the Sun, it is summer, and when it's angled away from the Sun, it's winter. In the southern hemisphere, December, January, and February are our summer months, so we get to enjoy the best of the summer produce—such as sweet, juicy tomatoes—during our holiday season!

PREPARA TU RELLENO FAVORITO (PREPARE YOUR FAVORITE FILLING)

You can customize the filling for your tomates rellenos by swapping in different ingredients for the rice, ham, and peas. Here are a few ideas.

Instead of cooked white rice, use **cooked brown rice, quinoa, barley, couscous,** or **cauliflower rice.**

Instead of chopped deli ham, use **chopped deli turkey, chopped cooked hot dogs, shredded cooked chicken,** or **canned tuna.**

Instead of peas, use **rinsed canned chickpeas, chopped green beans,** or **thawed frozen corn.**

ZAPALLITOS SALTEADOS

(STIR-FRIED ZUCCHINI)

"Zapallito" translates as "little pumpkin" or "little squash." The zapallitos I grew up eating in Argentina are called "zapallitos de tronco" ("stem squashes"). They're small, round, and bright green, with a flavor and texture similar to zucchini, which is easier to find in major American grocery stores. When I was in college, I also had a full-time job, which meant that I didn't have a lot of free time. Whenever I needed a quick,

inexpensive, and filling meal, I turned to zapallitos salteados (or zapallitos revueltos, which is when you add scrambled eggs—see the recipe on the right). Today, every time I cook this for dinner, it reminds me of my college days in Argentina. You can serve your zapallitos salteados with Arroz Blanco (page 154).

 **Argentina**

SERVES 4 to 6

DIFFICULTY LEVEL

¡EN SUS MARCAS! Ready!

INGREDIENTS

- 1 tablespoon **olive oil**
- 1 **red onion**, peeled and sliced thin (see page 19)
- 1 **red bell pepper**, stemmed, seeded, and sliced thin (see page 20)
- 3 **small zucchini**, sliced ¼ inch thick (about 3 cups)
- 2 teaspoons **kosher salt**
- ⅛ teaspoon **pepper**
- 1 **carrot**, peeled and shredded on the large holes of a box grater
- 2 teaspoons **dried oregano**
- ½ teaspoon **dried thyme**

¡LISTOS! Set!

EQUIPMENT

12-inch nonstick skillet with a lid

Rubber spatula

Oven mitts

¡FUERA! Go!

1. In a 12-inch nonstick skillet, heat the oil over medium-high heat for about 1 minute (the oil should be hot but not smoking). Add the onion and bell pepper and cook, stirring occasionally with a rubber spatula, until the vegetables are just beginning to soften, 3 to 5 minutes.

2. Stir in the zucchini, salt, and pepper and cook, stirring occasionally, for 3 minutes. Stir in the carrot, oregano, and thyme.

3. Cover the skillet with a lid; reduce the heat to medium-low; and cook until the zucchini is tender but still bright green, about 3 minutes. Turn off the heat. Use oven mitts to remove the lid. Serve.

ZAPALLITOS REVUELTOS (STIR-FRIED ZUCCHINI WITH SCRAMBLED EGGS)

If you like, add some scrambled eggs to your zapallitos salteados to turn them into zapallitos revueltos! Once the zucchini is tender in step 3, remove the lid and increase the heat to medium. Use a rubber spatula to push the vegetables to 1 side of the skillet. Add **3 large eggs**, beaten with a fork, to the empty side of the skillet. Let the eggs set for 30 seconds to 1 minute. Stir the eggs until they clump and are still slightly wet. Then, gently stir the eggs into the vegetables. Turn off the heat. Season with salt and pepper to taste. Serve.

MUCHÍSMOS ZAPALLITOS (SO MANY SQUASHES!)

Many squashes are native to Latin America, where they've been cultivated for thousands of years. (Archaeologists have even found 10,000-year-old squash remains at an archaeological site in México!) Today, you'll find a rainbow of colorful squashes of all shapes and sizes in markets across the region (though they go by different names in different countries). Some, such as green-skinned zapallo macre, are so huge that people typically buy just a chunk at a time. Others are long and skinny, such as the snakelike calabaza de serpiente. Or you might come across wrinkly skinned chayotes or green-and-white-speckled chilacayotes.

Guarniciones y Salsas
Sides and Sauces

FRIJOLES NEGROS
(BLACK BEANS)

México
SERVES 6 (Makes about 3 cups)
DIFFICULTY LEVEL

¡EN SUS MARCAS! Ready!

INGREDIENTS

1 cup **dried black beans**

1 quart **water**, plus extra for soaking

1 tablespoon **kosher salt**

1 **onion**, peeled and halved, with the root end still intact

2 **bay leaves**

¡LISTOS! Set!

EQUIPMENT

Rimmed baking sheet

Parchment paper

Colander

Large container or bowl

Ruler

Plastic wrap

Dutch oven with a lid

Spider skimmer or large spoon

Wooden spoon

Oven mitts

Serving bowl

When I was growing up, my family didn't eat many beans. It wasn't until I moved to the United States that I had my first memorable bean-eating experience, when I discovered black beans, cooked from scratch. I felt like, for the first time, I was tasting the real flavor of the beans and I loved their soft, slightly creamy texture. While cooking dried beans takes longer than just opening a can of beans, they are worth the wait. You can use these frijoles negros in Gallo Pinto (page 42) or Mis Nachos Favoritos (page 102) or you can serve them alongside Ropa Vieja (page 122) or with some Arroz Blanco (page 154). What is your favorite way to eat these frijoles? (Keep in mind that this recipe is a two-day project, so be sure to plan ahead.)

1. DAY 1: Line a rimmed baking sheet with parchment paper. Spread the beans on the parchment-lined baking sheet and remove any stones or pebbles that might have ended up in the bag (see the photo below). Transfer the beans to a colander and rinse them under cold running water, stirring with your fingers to remove any dirt.

2. Place the rinsed beans in a large container and cover them with at least 2 inches of water. Cover the container with plastic wrap, put it in the refrigerator, and let the beans soak for 24 hours. The beans will swell and double in size.

3. DAY 2: Drain the beans in a colander in the sink. Place the beans, water, salt, onion, and bay leaves in a Dutch oven. Bring the water to a boil over high heat. Use a spider skimmer to skim off and discard any foam that rises to the surface.

4. Reduce the heat to low and cover the pot with a lid. Simmer the beans, stirring occasionally with a wooden spoon and skimming off any foam that rises to the surface (use oven mitts to remove the lid), until the beans are tender, 45 minutes to 1 hour. (Make sure that you do not rapidly boil the beans—that will loosen their skins and you'll end up with broken, mushy beans. If your water starts boiling, use oven mitts to move the lid slightly to one side to release the steam.) Turn off the heat.

5. Ask a grown-up to drain the beans. Discard the onion and bay leaves. Transfer the beans to a serving bowl. Season with salt to taste and serve. (Beans can be refrigerated for up to 3 days.)

ASEGÚRATE QUE NO TENGAN PIEDRAS (MAKE SURE THE BEANS DON'T HAVE STONES)

Spread the beans on the parchment-lined baking sheet and remove any stones or pebbles that might have ended up in the bag. The easiest way is to slowly push the beans from one side of the baking sheet to the other as you look.

¿REMOJAS LOS FRIJOLES O NO? (DO YOU SOAK THE BEANS OR NOT?)

Different cooks have different opinions on whether you need to soak dried beans before you cook them. Some say that if your dried beans are "fresh" (meaning they've been dried very recently), you don't need to soak them. But without soaking, you'd have to cook the beans for much longer! During that long soak, the beans absorb some of the water—that's why they end up so much bigger at the end of the soaking process. The soaking sort of "jump-starts" the cooking, so it takes less time for the beans to absorb the hot water and turn fully tender as they simmer on the stove.

ARROZ BLANCO
(WHITE RICE)

Argentina
SERVES 4 (Makes about 2 cups)
DIFFICULTY LEVEL

¡EN SUS MARCAS! Ready!
●●·●●●●●●●●··●●●●

INGREDIENTS

1 cup **long-grain white rice**

2 cups **water**

¡LISTOS! Set!
●●●●●●●●·●●●●●·●●●

EQUIPMENT

Fine-mesh strainer

Medium bowl

Large saucepan with a tight-fitting lid

Oven mitts

Fork

As a kid, I was always in charge of making rice. My mom joked that it was a good thing I was born with a rice-cooking talent, because any time she cooked rice, it either turned out too dry or too soupy. In my opinion, cooking rice is one of those things where practice makes perfect—as long as you follow the basic steps in this recipe. It's a cooking technique that everyone should know how to do. (Though, if you turn out to be like my mom, you can always use a rice cooker, which I love, too!)

¡FUERA! Go!

●●●○●●○●●○●●●○●●●●○●

1. Rinse the rice in a fine-mesh strainer set over a medium bowl in the sink, following the photo on the right. (Make sure not to skip this step—unrinsed rice will cook up too sticky for this recipe!)

2. Transfer the rinsed rice to a large saucepan. Add the water, making sure that every grain is covered. Do not stir the rice and do not add salt! (I don't cook my rice with salt—this way it's like a blank canvas, so you can add lots of flavor later.)

3. Bring to a boil over medium-high heat. Reduce the heat to low; cover the pot with a lid (making sure that the lid is tight); and simmer gently until all the water is absorbed, 15 to 18 minutes. (Make sure to set a timer. And don't peek, stir, or shake the pot—the rice is now in control!)

4. Turn off the heat and carefully slide the saucepan to a cool burner. Let the rice sit, undisturbed, for 10 minutes. Use oven mitts to remove the lid. Fluff the rice with a fork and season with salt to taste. Serve.

CÓMO LAVAR EL ARROZ (HOW TO RINSE THE RICE)

Set a fine-mesh strainer over a bowl in the sink. Add the rice. Fill the bowl with cold water until it covers the rice. Stir the rice gently with your hand a few times, lift the strainer out of the water, and discard the cloudy water. Repeat rinsing the rice about 3 more times, until the water runs clear.

DOS CONSEJOS PARA COCINAR ARROZ (TWO TIPS FOR COOKING RICE)

Rinse your rice: I always, always rinse my white rice. As you rinse, some of the starch on the surface of the rice comes off. That is what makes the water look cloudy. If you didn't rinse that starch away, it would make the rice cook up sticky instead of fluffy. (You can give brown rice just a quick rinse to remove any dust. Each grain is surrounded by a coating called the bran, which makes the rice brown and also keeps the starch trapped inside the rice.)

Follow the recipe: It's also really important to use the right amount of water and rice to make sure that your final product isn't too firm or too soupy. I like to use 2 cups of water for every 1 cup of rice.

TOSTONES CON MOJO DE AJO

(FRIED GREEN PLANTAINS WITH GARLIC DIPPING SAUCE)

My first encounter with tostones, crispy double-fried green plantains, was back in 1996 at a tiny restaurant in New York City. It was called Brisas del Caribe and they served dishes from around the Caribbean. I usually only ordered a coffee to go, but one day I was hungry and it was cold outside, so I asked for something small to snack on. And what did I get? Tostones! I immediately fell in love and my quest to find the best ones continues to this day. I learned to

make my version of tostones by watching other chefs (and through lots of trial and error!). This recipe involves frying, so make sure that you have a grown-up close by to help. Mojo de ajo is traditionally made with bitter or sour orange juice (jugo de naranja agria), which can be hard to find in the United States. To replicate the flavor I like to combine orange, lime, and lemon juices. I love my mojo de ajo tangy and very garlicky!

 Puerto Rico

SERVES **4**

DIFFICULTY LEVEL

¡EN SUS MARCAS!  Ready!

INGREDIENTS

MOJO DE AJO

- ¼ cup **orange juice**, squeezed from ½ orange (see page 20)
- 2 tablespoons **lime juice**, squeezed from 1 lime (see page 20)
- 1½ tablespoons **lemon juice**, squeezed from ½ lemon (see page 20)
- 5 **garlic cloves**, peeled and minced (see page 19)
- 1½ teaspoons **olive oil**
- ½ teaspoon **dried oregano**
- ⅛ teaspoon **kosher salt**

TOSTONES

- 2 **green plantains**, peeled and each one cut crosswise (the short way) into 8 pieces (see page 41)
- 1 cup **vegetable oil** for frying

¡LISTOS!  Set!

EQUIPMENT

Small saucepan	Slotted spoon
Spoon	Fork
2-cup jar with a tight-fitting lid	Sturdy glass or a small wooden press (tostonera)
Serving platter	Ruler
Paper towels	
12-inch skillet	

¡FUERA!  Go!

1. For the mojo de ajo: Add all of the mojo de ajo ingredients to a small saucepan and stir with a spoon to combine.

2. Cook over low heat for 3 minutes (do not boil it). Turn off the heat. Let cool slightly and pour the mojo de ajo into a 2-cup jar. Let cool completely, about 20 minutes. (Mojo de ajo can be refrigerated for up to 3 days.)

3. For the tostones: Line a serving platter with paper towels and place it near the stovetop.

4. In a 12-inch skillet, heat the oil over medium-high heat for about 2 minutes (the oil should be hot but not smoking). Ask a grown-up to carefully add the plantains and fry until they start to turn light golden, about 1 minute. Use a slotted spoon and fork to carefully flip the plantains. Cook until the second side is light golden, about 1 minute.

5. Turn off the heat. Use the slotted spoon to transfer the plantains to the paper towel–lined platter to drain the oil. (Don't clean the skillet yet—you'll need it again!)

KEEP GOING

6. Using the bottom of a sturdy glass, smash and flatten the plantains until they are ⅛ to ¼ inch thick (see the photo on the right).

7. Heat the oil back up over medium-high heat for about 1 minute (the oil should be hot but not smoking). Ask a grown-up to carefully add half of the smashed plantains to the skillet. Cook until they're golden brown on the first side, 1 to 2 minutes.

8. Use a slotted spoon and fork to carefully flip the plantains. Cook until they're golden brown on the second side, 1 to 2 minutes. Transfer the plantains to the paper towel–lined platter and let drain.

9. Repeat frying with the remaining smashed plantains. Turn off the heat. Sprinkle the tostones with salt to taste. Serve warm with the mojo de ajo for dipping.

CÓMO APLASTAR LOS PLÁTANOS (HOW TO SMASH THE PLANTAINS)

Using the bottom of a sturdy glass or a small wooden press (tostonera), smash and flatten the plantains until they are ⅛ to ¼ inch thick. (Do this gently to keep the plantains from breaking apart! A few cracks around the edges are OK as long as the plantain stays in one piece. It's best to do this when the plantains are still warm.)

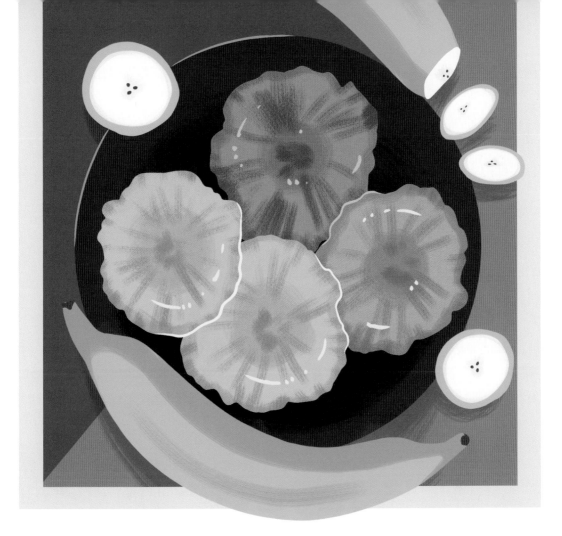

PLÁTANOS FRITOS DOS VECES

(GREEN PLANTAINS FRIED TWICE)

You'll find these crispy, double-fried plantains across Latin America, where they go by several different names, such as "fritos verdes" ("fried greens"), "patacones" (from the word for silver coins used in Colombia long ago), and "tostones" (from the Spanish word "tostar," which means "to toast," or possibly from "tostón," a 50-cent coin). They're especially popular in Puerto Rico, where they're served as a side dish or snack, often with mojo de ajo. Tostones are made with unripe, green plantains, which have a mild flavor and a starchy texture that's perfect for frying—twice! The first fry softens the sliced plantains just enough that you can smash them into disks, while the second fry gives them their golden-brown color and crisp texture.

MADUROS
(FRIED SWEET PLANTAINS)

I would eat maduros every day if I could—they are the ideal combination of salty and sweet (and they're delicious with a little bit of hot sauce, too!). This is another dish that you'll find across Latin America, from Cuba to the República Dominicana to Colombia, Ecuador, México, and many other countries. They're sometimes called "plátanos fritos" ("fried plantains") or "tajadas" ("slices"). Unlike tostones, which are made with firm, unripe green plantains, maduros are made with soft, sweet, ripe plantains ("maduro" means "ripe" or "mature"). I first learned how to make maduros from a Dominican friend. It's really important to use ripe plantains in this recipe! Make sure that the peels are mostly black and the plantains feel slightly soft when you gently squeeze them. To help plantains ripen more quickly, store them in a paper bag. This recipe involves frying, so make sure that you have a grown-up close by to help.

 República Dominicana

SERVES 4
DIFFICULTY LEVEL

¡EN SUS MARCAS! Ready!

●●●●●●●●●●●●●●●

INGREDIENTS

- 2 **ripe plantains**, peeled and each
  one cut crosswise (the short way)
  on the bias into 8 pieces
  (see page 41)

- ¾ cup **vegetable oil** for frying

¡LISTOS! Set!

●●●●●●●●●●●●●●●

EQUIPMENT

Serving platter

Paper towels

10-inch skillet

Slotted spoon

Fork

¡FUERA! Go!

●●●●●●●●●●●●●●●

1. Line a serving platter with paper towels and place it near the stovetop.

2. In a 10-inch skillet, heat the oil over medium heat for about 2 minutes (the oil should be hot but not smoking).

3. Ask a grown-up to carefully add half of the plantains to the skillet. Cook until the plantains are golden, 1 to 2 minutes.

4. Use a slotted spoon and fork to carefully flip the plantains (see the photo below). Cook until they are golden on the second side, about 1 minute.

5. Transfer the maduros to the paper towel–lined platter to drain. Repeat frying with the remaining plantains. Turn off the heat.

6. Sprinkle the maduros with salt to taste. Serve warm.

CÓMO DAR VUELTA A LOS PLÁTANOS (HOW TO FLIP THE PLANTAINS)

Use a slotted spoon and fork to carefully flip the plantains.

CÓMO MADURAN LOS PLÁTANOS (HOW PLANTAINS RIPEN)

Like bananas, as plantains ripen they turn from green to yellow to black and from firm to soft. At the same time, the plantains' starches slowly turn into sugars, making riper plantains much sweeter. It can take as long as a few weeks for a plantain to ripen from green to black.

Plantains can be cooked and eaten at all levels of ripeness. Green (unripe) plantains can be used to make tostones (page 156) or mangú (page 38). Yellow (half-ripe) plantains are often boiled or mashed, and black (ripe) plantains are used to make these maduros.

YUCA FRITA CON MAYONESA DE CILANTRO

(FRIED YUCA WITH CILANTRO MAYONNAISE)

Yuca frita ("fried yuca") is a fantastic alternative to french fries. Years ago, I used to babysit for a family from Panamá. The children's grandmother taught me how to make yuca frita. But yuca is not an easy vegetable to deal with—it's a big root that's hard to peel and chop. Luckily, nowadays you can find frozen, already-peeled yuca in the United States. Look for it in the frozen section of your grocery store—it might be labeled "yuca congelada" or "frozen cassava." This makes it much easier and faster to prepare yuca frita, and that means that you get to eat it sooner! This recipe involves frying, so make sure that you have a grown-up close by to help.

Panamá

SERVES 6

DIFFICULTY LEVEL

¡EN SUS MARCAS! Ready!

INGREDIENTS

YUCA

4 quarts **water**

1 tablespoon **kosher salt**

1 pound **frozen yuca**

1 cup **vegetable oil** for frying

MAYONESA DE CILANTRO

1 cup **cilantro leaves and stems**, roughly chopped (see page 19)

2 **garlic cloves**, peeled (see page 19)

½ cup **mayonnaise**

½ cup **sour cream**

3 tablespoons **lime juice**, squeezed from 2 limes (see page 20)

¡LISTOS! Set!

EQUIPMENT

Dutch oven	Cutting board
Tongs	Chef's knife
Wooden spoon	Ruler
Paring knife	Serving platter
Food processor	Paper towels
Rubber spatula	12-inch skillet
Medium bowl	Slotted spoon
Colander	Fork
Rimmed baking sheet	

¡FUERA!  Go!

1. For the yuca: In a Dutch oven, bring the water to a boil over high heat. Add the salt. Use tongs to carefully add the yuca to the boiling water (ask a grown-up for help). Cook, gently stirring occasionally with a wooden spoon, until the yuca is tender, 18 to 20 minutes (you can check for doneness by piercing the yuca with the tip of a paring knife—the knife should slide easily in and out of the yuca; ask a grown-up for help).

2. For the mayonesa de cilantro: While the yuca is cooking, add the cilantro and garlic to a food processor. Lock the lid into place. Hold down the pulse button for 1 second, then release. Repeat pulsing until the cilantro and garlic are finely chopped, ten to fifteen 1-second pulses. Remove the lid and carefully remove the processor blade (ask a grown-up for help).

3. Use a rubber spatula to scrape the chopped cilantro and garlic into a medium bowl. Stir in the mayonnaise, sour cream, and lime juice until the ingredients are well combined. Season with salt and pepper to taste. (The mayonesa de cilantro can be refrigerated for up to 3 days.)

KEEP GOING

4. When the yuca is ready, place a colander in the sink. Ask a grown-up to drain the yuca. Transfer the yuca to a rimmed baking sheet and spread the pieces out to prevent them from sticking to each other. Place the baking sheet in the refrigerator until the yuca is chilled and firm, about 15 minutes.

5. Transfer the yuca to a cutting board and use a chef's knife to cut it into smaller pieces following the photo below.

6. Line a serving platter with paper towels and place it near the stovetop. In a 12-inch skillet, heat the oil over medium-high heat for about 2 minutes (the oil should be hot but not smoking).

7. Ask a grown-up to carefully add half of the yuca pieces to the skillet. Fry the yuca until it is light golden, 2 to 4 minutes.

8. Use a slotted spoon and fork to carefully flip the yuca. Cook, turning as needed, until it is light golden all over, about 2 minutes.

9. Transfer the yuca frita to the paper towel–lined platter to drain. Repeat frying with the remaining yuca pieces. Turn off the heat. Sprinkle the yuca frita with salt to taste. Serve warm with the mayonesa de cilantro.

¿QUÉ ES LA YUCA? (WHAT IS YUCA?)

Yuca, also called manioc or cassava in English, and mandioca or aipim in Brazilian Portuguese, is a root vegetable that grows in tropical climates. Yucas have thick brown skins and starchy, slightly stringy white or light-yellow flesh. Amazingly, these vegetables can last underground for as long as three years before harvesting! Yucas are prepared many different ways in Latin American cuisine: They can be boiled, mashed, fried, grated, and even dried and ground into a kind of flour. This flour is used to make pan de yuca (yuca bread), which is known as pão de queijo (cheese bread) in Brasil.

CÓMO CORTAR LA YUCA EN PEDAZOS MÁS PEQUEÑOS (HOW TO CUT YUCA INTO SMALLER PIECES)

Transfer the yuca to a cutting board and use a chef's knife to cut it into smaller pieces that are 2 to 3 inches long and ½ to ¾ inch thick, removing any stringy pieces that look like twine.

HUEVOS FRITOS
(FRIED EGGS)

You can eat your fried eggs the way I did growing up—with bread on the side to dunk in the runny yolk—or serve them as part of Mangú con Los Tres Golpes (page 38) or Chilaquiles Verdes (page 44). As you are frying your eggs, there will be some splattering oil, so having a grown-up close by is a good idea!

Argentina
SERVES **4**
DIFFICULTY LEVEL

¡EN SUS MARCAS! Ready!
●●●●●●●●●●●●●●●

INGREDIENTS

4 **large eggs**

2 tablespoons **olive oil**

Flake sea salt

¡LISTOS! Set!
●●●●●●●●●●●●●●●

EQUIPMENT

4 small ramekins or bowls

12-inch nonstick skillet

Spatula

Serving plates

¡FUERA! Go!
●●●●●●●●●●●●●●●

1. Crack the eggs into the 4 small ramekins (1 egg per ramekin). Wash your hands.

2. In a 12-inch nonstick skillet, heat the oil over medium-high heat until it starts to shimmer, 30 seconds to 1 minute.

3. Carefully pour the eggs into the skillet. Do not shake the pan. Cook until the egg whites are almost completely white, 1 to 2 minutes. (If the oil splatters a little bit, you can watch the eggs from a safe distance; ask a grown-up for help.)

4. Reduce the heat to medium and cook until the whites are set and their edges start to turn golden brown, 1 to 2 minutes. Turn off the heat and slide the skillet to a cool burner.

5. Use a spatula to transfer the eggs to serving plates. Season with flake sea salt to taste. Serve.

~~~~~~~~~~~~~~~~~~~~~~~~~~~~~~~~~~~~~

EL SECRETO PARA ROMPER LOS HUEVOS (THE SECRET TO CRACKING EGGS)

Cracking eggs can be supereasy once you master this technique! I always crack my eggs on a flat surface, not on the side of a bowl. The flat surface will prevent little pieces of shell from going inward when you crack the egg. If a little piece of shell does wind up in your egg, do not worry—and do not try to pick it up with your fingers! Instead, use the biggest piece of shell that you have to scoop out the little piece—much easier!

CURTIDO
(CABBAGE SLAW)

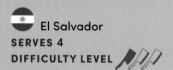 El Salvador

SERVES 4

DIFFICULTY LEVEL

¡EN SUS MARCAS! Ready!

●●•●•●●●●●●•●•●●●

INGREDIENTS

3 cups shredded **red cabbage** (see the photo on the right)

2 **carrots**, peeled and shredded (see the photo on the right)

1 **small red onion**, peeled and sliced thin (see page 19)

4 cups **boiling water**

½ cup **distilled white vinegar**

2 teaspoons **dried oregano**

1 teaspoon **kosher salt**

¡LISTOS! Set!

●●●●●●●●•●●●●●●•●●●●

EQUIPMENT

Large heatproof bowl

Colander

Slotted spoon

The first time I had curtido was at a neighbor's birthday party here in Jersey City. After that first taste, I started asking every Salvadoran I met for their recipe. I have always loved vinegary things, so it makes sense that I also love curtido. Soaking the vegetables in the boiling water softens them and makes it easier to squeeze out some of their water. It also allows them to better absorb the tangy vinegar. This is my version of a typical Salvadoran curtido that is served alongside Pupusas (page 62). If you don't have a food processor, grate the carrots on the large holes of a box grater and thinly slice the red cabbage.

¡FUERA! Go!

●●●◌●◌●◌●◌●◌●●◌●●●●●●

1. Combine cabbage, carrots, and onion in a large heatproof bowl. Ask a grown-up to pour the boiling water over the vegetables in the large bowl. Let it sit for 5 minutes.

2. Place a colander in the sink. Drain the vegetables well in the colander, pressing on them with a slotted spoon to remove as much excess water as possible.

3. Transfer the vegetables back to the now-empty bowl. Add the vinegar, oregano, and salt, and stir until the ingredients are well combined. Place the bowl in the refrigerator for at least 20 minutes before serving. (Curtido can be refrigerated in an airtight container for up to 4 days.)

❝❝ IT WAS VERY CRUNCHY GOOD."

—Benjamin, age 9

CÓMO RALLAR EL REPOLLO Y LAS ZANAHORIAS EN UN PROCESADOR DE ALIMENTOS (HOW TO SHRED THE CABBAGE AND CARROTS IN A FOOD PROCESSOR)

Put the shredding disk in place in the food processor. With the food processor running, work in small batches and place large pieces of the cabbage and peeled carrots in the feed tube and use the plastic pusher to guide the carrots or cabbage into the machine (ask a grown-up for help).

MORADO Y NARANJA (PURPLE AND ORANGE)

Honestly, I think the first thing that caught my eye about curtido was the colors. Purple and orange are two of my favorite colors, especially when they're next to one another. (Yes, I know: Red cabbage and red onions are actually PURPLE!) Orange carrots get their vibrant orange color from a pigment called beta-carotene (the same pigment that gives sweet potatoes and cantaloupe their color). Molecules called anthocyanins give red cabbage plus other blue-purple produce, such as blueberries and cherries, their purple hue.

CEBOLLAS EN VINAGRE
(PICKLED ONIONS)

I think pickled onions are a perfect tangy topping for tacos, tostones, maduros, and more, but my favorite way to eat them is with Mangú con los Tres Golpes (page 38)—that is why I say this recipe is from the República Dominicana! (Although cebollas en vinagre are eaten in lots of Latin American countries.) They are simple to make and are ready after sitting in the vinegar mixture for just 30 minutes. In my version, I use a few black peppercorns for flavoring, but you can swap them for other seasonings, such as ⅛ teaspoon of fennel seeds, mustard seeds, or coriander seeds. Red onions are my favorite onions to pickle because they turn bright pink, but you can use any onion you like for this recipe. If you'd like sweeter cebollas en vinagre, use cider vinegar instead of distilled white vinegar.

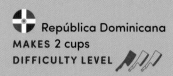

República Dominicana

MAKES 2 cups

DIFFICULTY LEVEL

¡EN SUS MARCAS! Ready!

INGREDIENTS

1 cup **water**

1 cup **distilled white vinegar**

1 teaspoon **kosher salt**

1 teaspoon **sugar**

1 **small red onion**, peeled and sliced thin (see page 19)

⅛ teaspoon **whole black peppercorns**

¡LISTOS! Set!

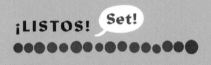

EQUIPMENT

Small saucepan

Spoon

Medium heatproof bowl

Slotted spoon

2-cup jar with a tight-fitting lid

Ladle

¡FUERA! Go!

1. In a small saucepan combine the water, vinegar, salt, and sugar. Bring to a simmer over medium heat and cook, stirring with a spoon, until the sugar dissolves, about 3 minutes. Turn off the heat.

2. Place the sliced onions in a medium heatproof bowl. Carefully pour the water-vinegar mixture over the onions. Let them sit for 10 minutes.

3. Use a slotted spoon to transfer the onions to a 2-cup jar. Add the black peppercorns. Use a ladle to pour the liquid into the jar to cover the onions (you may not need all of the liquid; discard any extra). Cover the jar tightly with a lid and give it a shake.

4. Refrigerate the cebollas en vinagre for at least 20 minutes before serving. (The cebollas en vinagre can be refrigerated for up to 2 weeks.)

CEBOLLAS QUE CAMBIAN DE COLOR (ONIONS THAT CHANGE COLOR)

My favorite part of making this recipe is watching the onions turn from purple to pink! Just like red cabbage, red onions get their purple color from molecules called anthocyanins. When anthocyanins meet acidic ingredients, such as vinegar, lime juice, or lemon juice, a chemical reaction takes place, turning them from deep purple to bright pink.

PICO DE GALLO
(CHOPPED FRESH SALSA)

Sometimes called "salsa fresca" ("fresh salsa"), "salsa cruda" ("raw salsa"), or "salsa bandera" ("flag salsa," because it includes the colors of the Mexican flag: green, white, and red), pico de gallo is one of the most popular condiments in México. It's a simple, no-cook sauce and nearly every version includes the same basic ingredients: chopped tomatoes, onion, chiles, lime juice, and cilantro. Serve your pico de gallo with Tacos de Carne Molida (page 84), Tostadas de Frijoles y Queso (page 104), Mis Nachos Favoritos (page 102), scrambled eggs, or with tortilla chips for scooping.

¡FUERA! **Go!**
●●●○●●●●○●●○●●○●●●

1. Combine all the ingredients in a medium bowl. Stir gently with a spoon until the ingredients are well combined.

2. Place in the refrigerator for at least 15 minutes. Season with salt to taste. Serve. (Pico de gallo can be refrigerated in an airtight container for up to 2 days.)

~~~~~~~~~~~~~~~~~~~~~~

TOMATES VIAJEROS (TRAVELING TOMATOES)

While today Italy may be famous for its tomato sauce, did you know that before the 1500s, there were no tomatoes in Europe? That's right! Tomatoes are native to Latin America, where they've been harvested by Indigenous peoples for more than a thousand years—the word "tomato" comes from the Nahuatl word "tomatl." (Nahuatl is a group of languages spoken by Indigenous peoples of México and Central America.) The Spanish conquistadores brought tomato seeds back to Europe, but tomatoes didn't become a part of European cuisines for a few more centuries, until pizza became popular in Naples in the 1800s.

México
MAKES **about 3 cups**
DIFFICULTY LEVEL

¡EN SUS MARCAS! **Ready!**
●●○●○●●●●●●●○●●●●

INGREDIENTS

- 6 **plum tomatoes**, cored, seeded, and cut into ¼-inch pieces (see page 67)
- 1 **onion**, peeled and chopped fine (see page 19)
- 1 **jalapeño chile**, stemmed, seeded, ribs removed, and chopped fine (see page 21)
- ½ cup minced **fresh cilantro** (see page 19)
- ¼ cup **lime juice**, squeezed from 2 limes (see page 20)
- ¾ teaspoon **kosher salt**

¡LISTOS! **Set!**
●●●●●●○●●●●●●●○●●●●

EQUIPMENT

Medium bowl

Spoon

UN MISTERIO CULINARIO (A CULINARY MYSTERY)

There are several theories about how this salsa got its name. Since "pico de gallo" means "rooster's beak," some believe the name refers to how the salsa was originally eaten: using your thumb and forefinger. Go ahead, try it! Does your hand look like a rooster's beak? Others believe the rooster connection comes from how the colors in the salsa match the colors in a rooster's feathers and comb. And yet another rooster-centric theory suggests that the finely chopped ingredients resemble small pieces of food farmers feed their roosters. Another possibility? "Pico de gallo" comes from the verb "picar," which can mean "to mince." Which do you think is the real story?

CHIMICHURRI
(CHIMICHURRI SAUCE)

You are very lucky: I am giving you the recipe for my mom's chimichurri, the one that I grew up eating. It is the best chimichurri you will ever have! You MUST serve chimichurri when you have Argentinean asado, our barbecue (see Entraña al Horno con Chimichurri, page 132). You can present your meat drizzled with the chimichurri, but it's most commonly served on the side, in a gravy boat or a jar, so that each person can add as much as they like to their plate. In Argentina, parsley is the main ingredient in chimichurri, but in some other countries they use cilantro as well. The food processor makes it easy to finely chop the parsley and garlic, but do not use it to mix the other ingredients into your sauce! That would give you an emulsified chimichurri when what you really want is to see the bits of herbs and spices floating in the oil.

 Argentina

MAKES **2 cups**

DIFFICULTY LEVEL

INGREDIENTS

- 3 cups **fresh parsley leaves**
- 4–5 **garlic cloves**, peeled (see page 19)
- 1 cup **olive oil**, plus extra as needed
- 2 tablespoons **lemon juice**, squeezed from 1 lemon (see page 20)
- 1 tablespoon **red wine vinegar**
- 1 teaspoon **dried oregano**
- ⅛–¼ teaspoon **red pepper flakes**
- ½ teaspoon **kosher salt**
- ⅛ teaspoon **pepper**
- 1 **bay leaf**

EQUIPMENT

Food processor

Rubber spatula

Medium bowl

2-cup jar with a tight-fitting lid

1. Add the parsley and garlic to a food processor. Lock the lid into place. Hold down the pulse button for 1 second, then release. Repeat pulsing until the parsley and garlic are finely chopped, about fifteen 1-second pulses. Remove the lid and carefully remove the processor blade (ask a grown-up for help).

2. Use a rubber spatula to transfer the chopped parsley and garlic to a medium bowl. Add the oil, lemon juice, vinegar, oregano, red pepper flakes, salt, and pepper. Stir until the ingredients are well combined. Season with salt and pepper to taste.

3. Transfer the chimichurri to a 2-cup jar. Add the bay leaf. If all the ingredients are not covered in oil, add extra oil to cover. Cover the jar tightly with a lid. Give it a nice shake and refrigerate the chimichurri until ready to use. Bring to room temperature before serving. Just make sure you don't eat the bay leaf! (Chimichurri can be refrigerated for up to 4 days.)

CÓMO MANTENER EL CHIMICHURRI FRESCO POR MÁS TIEMPO (HOW TO KEEP YOUR CHIMICHURRI FRESH LONGER)

Chimichurri adds lots of flavor to your asado, and it also adds lots of color! To keep your chimichurri as green as possible, make sure that all of the solids in your sauce are fully covered by a layer of olive oil. If you left the chopped parsley exposed to air, it would oxidize—the oxygen in the air would trigger a chemical reaction that turns it from bright green to dull, brownish-green pretty quickly. Covering the parsley with a layer of olive oil blocks a lot of the oxygen from reaching it, so it oxidizes more slowly and your chimichurri stays greener for longer.

ENSALADA MIXTA
(MIXED GREEN SALAD)

In Argentina, ensalada mixta is traditionally served as a side during an asado (our barbecue) because it's an easy way to add some crunchy, refreshing vegetables to all of that grilled meat! The most classic combination is lettuce, tomatoes, and onion, with a simple oil and vinegar dressing. When I was growing up, the men were in charge of grilling the meat at many asados and the women were in charge of making the side dishes and salads, including the ensalada mixta. My mom did not like this (and neither did I!), so from an early age she showed my brother and me how to do both—and that is the way it should be! But ensalada mixta isn't just popular at asados—when you have lunch at any bistro restaurant in Buenos Aires, you do not order an "ensalada," you order a "mixta."

Argentina

SERVES 4

DIFFICULTY LEVEL

¡EN SUS MARCAS! Ready!

INGREDIENTS

1 **medium head green leaf** or **romaine lettuce**, cut crosswise (the short way) into ½-inch-thick strips

3 **plum tomatoes**, cored and chopped into ½-inch pieces (see page 67)

1 **small red onion**, peeled and sliced thin (see page 19)

3 tablespoons **olive oil**

1 tablespoon **red wine vinegar**

⅛ teaspoon **kosher salt**

¡LISTOS! Set!

EQUIPMENT

Serving bowl

Tongs

¡FUERA! Go!

In a serving bowl, combine the lettuce, tomatoes, and onion. Drizzle the oil and vinegar over top and sprinkle with the salt. Use tongs to toss until the ingredients are combined. Season with salt to taste. Serve.

CÓMO LAVAR Y SECAR LA LECHUGA (HOW TO WASH AND DRY LETTUCE)

There are so many varieties of lettuce at grocery stores and farmers' markets: romaine, Bibb, green leaf, red leaf, loose-leaf, butterhead, little gem, crisphead, oak leaf . . . I promise I am not making up these names! I love them all, and you can choose your favorite for this ensalada mixta. But no matter which lettuce you use, it's important to wash your lettuce to remove any soil and then dry the leaves thoroughly by laying them out on a clean dish towel. (If your lettuce is too wet, you'll end up with a very soggy salad!) To cut your lettuce, you can use a knife to chop it, or you can use your hands to tear the leaves into small pieces.

❝ TART AND TASTY.❞

—Maya, age 10

ÁRBOL DE NAVIDAD DE ENSALADA RUSA

(RUSSIAN SALAD CHRISTMAS TREE)

This is my mom's Christmas version of ensalada rusa—a potato salad—that is shaped into a Christmas tree and decorated with "ornaments" made from colorful cut-out carrots and radishes. My brother and I loved when she would make this when we were growing up—and my mom loved to make it for us! (If it is not Christmas time, or if you do not celebrate Christmas, ensalada rusa

is equally delicious served in a large bowl.) To quickly thaw the frozen carrots and peas, place them in a heatproof bowl and cover them with boiling water. Let them sit for 3 minutes to warm through and then drain them in a colander in the sink. Potatoes can be difficult to prep—because they're starchy, they can easily stick to your knife. Be sure to ask a grown-up to help you cut them.

 **Argentina**

SERVES 8 to 10

DIFFICULTY LEVEL

¡EN SUS MARCAS! Ready!

INGREDIENTS

- 2 pounds **russet potatoes**, peeled and cut into ½-inch pieces
- 1 tablespoon **kosher salt**
- 20 ounces **frozen cubed carrots and peas**, thawed (see the note on the left)
- 2 cups **mayonnaise**
- ¼ cup **lemon juice**, squeezed from 2 lemons (see page 20)
- 1 tablespoon **olive oil**
- ¼ cup chopped **fresh parsley** (see page 19)
- 1 **purple carrot**, peeled and sliced ¼ inch thick
- 1 **yellow** or **orange carrot**, peeled and sliced ¼ inch thick
- 1 **watermelon radish**, trimmed and sliced ¼ inch thick

¡LISTOS! Set!

EQUIPMENT

Large saucepan	Plastic wrap
Ruler	Large, flat serving platter
Paring knife	
Colander	Small star cutter (optional)
Rimmed baking sheet	Small round cutter (optional)
Large bowl	
Rubber spatula	

¡FUERA! Go!

1. Put the potatoes in a large saucepan. Add water to cover the potatoes by 1 inch. Add the salt. Bring to a boil over medium-high heat. Cook until the potatoes are tender and cooked through but not falling apart, about 5 to 7 minutes (you can check for doneness by piercing the potatoes with the tip of a paring knife—the knife should slide easily in and out of the potatoes; ask a grown-up for help).

2. Place a colander in the sink. Ask a grown-up to drain the potatoes. Run cold water over the potatoes briefly, and drain well. Transfer the potatoes to a rimmed baking sheet and spread into an even layer. Refrigerate the potatoes until they are cool to the touch, about 15 minutes.

3. Place the potatoes and thawed carrots and peas in a large bowl. Add the mayonnaise, lemon juice, and oil and gently stir with a rubber spatula until the ingredients are combined, making sure not to turn your potatoes into mush! Season with salt and pepper to taste. Cover with plastic wrap and refrigerate until cold, 30 minutes to 1 hour.

4. Form the ensalada rusa into a Christmas tree on a large, flat serving platter following the photos on page 180. Serve cold.

KEEP GOING

Depending on how much time she had, my mom might make her ensalada rusa Christmas tree a little differently. Some years she made just one big triangle with a little trunk (if she was short on time!), while in other years, the tree was shaped by three smaller triangles. She would use special plastic cutters to make shapes out of carrots for the "ornaments"—since they weren't that sharp, my mom used to cook the carrots a little bit first to soften them. We would help her cut out the shapes while we munched on the leftover carrots. If you have small cutters, you can also cut out shapes to decorate your tree. Make sure that your hands are clean or you wear disposable gloves when forming the tree—it's a messy job!

1. Transfer about ⅓ of the chilled ensalada rusa to the top of a large, flat serving platter. Use your hands to shape the ensalada rusa into a triangle, forming the top of the tree. Repeat with remaining ensalada rusa to form two more triangles.

2. Decorate the Christmas tree with chopped parsley, sliced carrots, and sliced radishes. Use slices of carrot or radish to form the tree trunk.

¡ESTA ENSALADA HA VIAJADO MUCHO!

(THIS SALAD HAS TRAVELED A LOT!)

Ensalada rusa ("Russian salad"), unsurprisingly, has its roots in Russia, where it is called "Olivier salad." It is named after chef Lucien Olivier, who served a fancy version of it at Moscow's Hermitage Restaurant in the late 1800s. Over time, immigrants brought a simpler version of the salad westward, across Europe and eventually to Spain, where it is called "ensaladilla rusa" ("little Russian salad"). The Spanish eventually brought it to Latin America, where it's a popular holiday dish. Different countries and even different families add different ingredients to their ensaladas rusas, such as hard-boiled eggs, beets, cooked shrimp or chicken, sausage, or pickles, but it always has its signature mayonnaise-based dressing!

Postre
Dessert

CHOCOTORTA

(NO-BAKE CHOCOLATE COOKIE AND DULCE DE LECHE LAYER CAKE)

 Argentina

SERVES 8

DIFFICULTY LEVEL

¡EN SUS MARCAS! Ready!

●●●•●●●●●●●•●●●●

INGREDIENTS

- 3 cups **dulce de leche**
- 3 cups **sour cream**
- 3 (8.8-ounce) packs **Chocolinas Cookies** (about 90 cookies) (or any chocolate tea biscuits)
- 2 cups (16 ounces) brewed **coffee**, cooled (or milk or chocolate milk)
- **Sprinkles** (optional)

¡LISTOS! Set!

●●●●●●●●●●●●●•●●●

EQUIPMENT

- 2 medium bowls
- Rubber spatula
- 2-cup liquid measuring cup
- 8-inch square baking dish
- Dry measuring cups
- Small offset (icing) spatula
- Large zipper-lock plastic bag
- Rolling pin
- Chef's knife
- Spatula

This supereasy recipe is what every child I know in Argentina wants for their birthday. It's basically a cake made out of chocolate cookies and filled with dulce de leche and sour cream . . . what's not to like? When I was growing up, my abuela made our birthday cakes from scratch, so I had chocotorta only at friends' houses. (Once, my mom made me one, but kept it a secret from my abuela—don't tell!) In this recipe, the coffee can be replaced by milk or chocolate milk (or even just decaf coffee). If you don't have sour cream, you can substitute mascarpone, whipped cream cheese, or crème fraîche. Note that this cake chills for 4 to 24 hours.

1. In a medium bowl, combine the dulce de leche and sour cream. Use a rubber spatula to stir until well combined and no swirls of color remain, making sure to scrape the bottom of the bowl.

2. Carefully open the packages of cookies and put the cookies in the second medium bowl. Don't worry if some are broken—you will need them to fill gaps in the layers and for the topping. Pour the coffee into a 2-cup liquid measuring cup.

3. Working with 1 cookie at a time, dip the cookie in the coffee and place in an 8-inch square baking dish. (Dip the cookie for only a second so that it does not get too soggy and fall apart.)

4. Repeat dipping cookies to create 1 single layer of cookies in the bottom of the baking dish. (The cookies can overlap—just press them gently together.)

5. Dollop 1½ cups dulce de leche mixture over the soaked cookies. Use a small offset (icing) spatula to spread into an even layer, making sure to go to the edges of the baking dish.

6. Repeat soaking and layering 3 more times with the remaining cookies and dulce de leche mixture—there should be 4 of each layer total! You should have some unsoaked cookies left over.

7. Place the remaining unsoaked cookies into a large zipper-lock plastic bag. Seal the bag, making sure to press out all the air. Use a rolling pin to gently pound the bag to crush the cookies into tiny pieces.

8. Sprinkle the crushed cookie pieces and sprinkles (if using) over the top dulce de leche layer. Place the baking dish in the refrigerator. Let the chocotorta chill for at least 4 hours or up to 24 hours.

9. Use a chef's knife to cut the chocotorta into pieces. Use a spatula to serve. (The chocotorta can be refrigerated for up to 2 days.)

¡PRUÉBALA HELADA TAMBIÉN! (TRY IT FROZEN, TOO!)

I really don't know anybody who has kept leftovers of this cake for very long . . . it's too delicious! But if you do have any leftovers or are thinking ahead to a cold summer treat, you can freeze pieces of this cake for later. (Wrap each piece well in plastic wrap first.) When you eat the frozen chocotorta, it will taste like ice cream cake! Just let it thaw in the fridge for a few minutes before biting into it.

PASTEL DE TRES LECHES CON COCO

(THREE MILKS CAKE WITH COCONUT)

 México

SERVES 12

DIFFICULTY LEVEL

¡EN SUS MARCAS! Ready!

INGREDIENTS

- 1 box **yellow cake mix**, baked in a 13-by-9-inch metal baking pan following the package instructions and cooled completely
- 1 cup **sweetened condensed milk**
- 1 cup **evaporated milk**
- 1 cup **canned coconut milk**
- 1 cup cold **heavy cream**
- 1 teaspoon **vanilla extract**
- ½ cup **shredded unsweetened coconut flakes** or 1 cup **Dang coconut chips**

¡LISTOS! Set!

EQUIPMENT

13-by-9-inch metal baking pan

4-cup liquid measuring cup

Rubber spatula

Skewer

Medium bowl

Electric mixer

Offset (icing) spatula

Chef's knife

Spatula

The first time I heard about tres leches cake, a dish popular in México that involves soaking a cake in a combination of tres leches (three types of milk), I was . . . incredulous. I'm not a huge fan of mushy foods. But I AM a huge fan of using a leftover cake and turning it into something delicioso. So I gave it a try. And now I am hooked. Because a tres leches cake isn't mushy—it's perfectly moist. In my family-style version, I use a boxed cake mix (yes, a boxed cake mix!) and a combo of condensed milk, evaporated milk, and coconut milk. For serving, I don't remove the cake from the pan in which it's baked. It's much easier and more homey to serve it straight from the pan! Note that this cake chills for 4 to 24 hours.

1. In a 4-cup liquid measuring cup, combine the condensed milk, evaporated milk, and coconut milk. Use a rubber spatula to stir until well combined.

2. Use a skewer to poke lots of holes all over the cooled cake (see the photos below) (make sure the cake is completely cool before you add the milk mixture). Very slowly pour the milk mixture evenly all over the cake. (The milk mixture will run to the sides, but that's OK!)

3. Place the baking pan uncovered in the refrigerator. Let the cake chill for at least 4 hours or up to 24 hours. (The longer it sits, the better it will taste!)

4. When you are ready to serve the cake, pour the cold cream and vanilla into a medium bowl. Use an electric mixer on low speed to whip the cream until it starts getting foamy, about 2 minutes. Increase the speed to medium-high and whip until the cream gets light and fluffy and holds its shape in soft peaks, 1 to 2 minutes.

5. Use an offset (icing) spatula to spread the whipped cream evenly over the cake. Sprinkle the shredded coconut flakes over top. Use a chef's knife to cut the cake into pieces. Use a spatula to serve. (The cake can be refrigerated for up to 2 days—although I do not think it will last that long!)

CÓMO REMOJAR EL PASTEL (HOW TO SOAK THE CAKE)

1. Use a skewer to poke lots of holes all over the cooled cake.

2. Very, VERY slowly pour the milk mixture all over the cake.

ALFAJORES DE MAICENA

(SANDWICH COOKIES WITH DULCE DE LECHE)

Alfajores are sweet treats popular in Argentina: two buttery, crumbly cookies, often with a layer of dulce de leche in between them. Some types of alfajores are covered in chocolate or powdered sugar, while alfajores de maicena are left "naked" with a bit of shredded coconut on the sides. There are variations filled with membrillo (quince) paste, apple butter, figs, lemon, and more. "Maicena" means "cornstarch," a key ingredient in this recipe, hence their name. The tiny ones are called "alfajorcitos." For kids in Argentina, there is no birthday party without them; they are sold at every bakery and at every school cafeteria. But in my opinion, the best ones are always the ones you bake at home. My recipe is filled with dulce de leche and coated in shredded coconut and is as Argentinean as my accent!

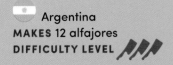 Argentina

MAKES 12 alfajores

DIFFICULTY LEVEL

¡EN SUS MARCAS! Ready!

INGREDIENTS

- 8 tablespoons **unsalted butter**, cut into 8 pieces and softened
- ½ cup (2 ounces) **confectioners' (powdered) sugar**
- 2 **large eggs**, plus 1 **large egg white**
- 1 tablespoon grated **lemon zest** (zested from 1 lemon) (see page 20)
- 1 teaspoon **vanilla extract**
- 1½ cups plus 2 tablespoons (6½ ounces) **cornstarch**, plus extra for shaping
- ¾ cup (3¾ ounces) **all-purpose flour**, sifted (see page 21), plus extra for the counter
- 1 teaspoon **baking powder**
- Pinch **kosher salt**
- 2 cups **dulce de leche**
- 1 cup **unsweetened shredded coconut**

¡LISTOS! Set!

EQUIPMENT

Stand mixer with a paddle attachment	2-inch round cutter
Rubber spatula	Small offset (icing) spatula
Plastic wrap	Oven mitts
Rimmed baking sheet	Cooling rack
Parchment paper	Spatula
Rolling pin	1-tablespoon measuring spoon
Ruler	

¡FUERA! Go!

1. In the bowl of a stand mixer, combine the softened butter and confectioners' sugar. Lock the bowl into place and attach the paddle to the stand mixer. Start the mixer on low speed and beat until creamy and combined, about 1 minute.

2. Increase the speed to medium and continue beating until well combined, about 2 minutes. Stop the mixer. Use a rubber spatula to scrape down the bowl.

3. Start the mixer on medium speed and add the whole eggs, one at a time, and beat until well combined, about 1 minute. Add the egg white, lemon zest, and vanilla and continue beating until well combined, about 1 minute. Stop the mixer and scrape down the bowl.

4. Add the cornstarch. Start the mixer on low speed and beat until just combined, about 1 minute. Increase the speed to medium-high and beat until well incorporated, about 1 minute. Stop the mixer and scrape down the bowl.

5. Add the flour, baking powder, and salt. Start the mixer and beat on low speed for 1 minute. Increase the speed to medium-high and beat until dough forms (like play dough!), about 2 minutes. Stop the mixer.

6. Scrape down the bowl and remove the bowl from the mixer. Cover the bowl with plastic wrap and place in the refrigerator until the dough is chilled, about 1 hour.

KEEP GOING

7. Line a rimmed baking sheet with parchment paper. Sprinkle extra flour on a clean counter. Divide the dough into 2 equal pieces. Working with 1 piece at a time, transfer the dough to the floured counter and knead briefly until the dough is no longer sticky. Roll the dough into a 10-inch-wide circle, about ⅛ to ¼ inch thick.

8. Dip a 2-inch round cutter into extra cornstarch. Cut out 12 cookies from the round of dough and use a small offset (icing) spatula to transfer them to the parchment-lined baking sheet. Make sure to dip the cutter in cornstarch each time you cut out a cookie. Repeat kneading, rolling, and cutting with the second piece of dough—you should have 24 cookies total.

9. Place the baking sheet in the refrigerator until cookies are chilled, about 20 minutes.

10. While the dough chills, adjust an oven rack to the middle position and heat the oven to 350 degrees.

11. Place the baking sheet in the oven. Bake until the cookies puff a little, 8 to 10 minutes. (The cookies will be pale, not browned.)

12. Use oven mitts to remove the baking sheet from the oven and place on a cooling rack (ask a grown-up for help). Let the cookies cool on the baking sheet for 5 minutes. Use a spatula to carefully transfer the cookies directly to the cooling rack. Let the cookies cool completely, about 20 minutes.

13. Assemble 12 alfajores with dulce de leche and coat the sides with shredded coconut following the photos on the far right. Serve.

¿POR QUÉ MAICENA? (WHY CORNSTARCH?)

They are called alfajores de maicena for a reason. "Maicena" translates as "cornstarch," and cornstarch is a key ingredient in these crumbly cookies. Why? Cornstarch is a white, powdery starch that comes from corn. It absorbs liquid and won't form any gluten, the protein that gives breads and cookies made with wheat flour their structure. Using cornstarch in addition to flour gives us supertender cookies, ones that practically melt in your mouth . . . the perfect texture to go alongside thick and creamy dulce de leche!

CÓMO ARMAR LOS ALFAJORES (HOW TO ASSEMBLE ALFAJORES)

1. Flip 12 of the cookies over. Scoop 1 tablespoon dulce de leche into the center of each flipped cookie. Place a second cookie on top of the filling to create 12 alfajores, pressing gently until the filling reaches the edges of the cookies.

2. Put the shredded coconut on a small plate. Gently roll each alfajor on its side in the coconut until the sides are completely covered.

 THE COOKIE HAD A VERY GOOD BALANCE OF LEMON FLAVOR AND DULCE DE LECHE."

—Keira, age 13

ARROZ CON LECHE
(RICE PUDDING)

When I was growing up, my abuela made a lot of arroz con leche, or rice pudding, and my whole family loved it. The creamy, starchy white rice absorbs the milk, sugar, and spices and makes the whole house smell sweet. This is a classic dish that's made slightly differently in every country where it's popular—with cinnamon in México and nutmeg in Costa Rica. We always used orange zest, vanilla, and cinnamon. I prefer to use jasmine rice in this recipe, but you can use any long-grain white rice. You want your arroz con leche to be creamy—not solid—so make sure that you don't cook it for too long! Note that this arroz con leche chills for at least 8 hours or up to 3 days.

 Argentina

SERVES 8

DIFFICULTY LEVEL

INGREDIENTS

- 1 cup **water**
- ½ cup **jasmine rice**
- ⅛ teaspoon **kosher salt**
- 2 cups **milk**
- ¼ cup **sugar**
- 2 (3-inch-long) strips **orange zest**
- ¼ teaspoon **vanilla extract**
- **Ground cinnamon** (optional)
- Grated **orange zest** (optional) (see page 20)

¡LISTOS! Set!

EQUIPMENT

Large heavy-bottomed saucepan with a lid

Oven mitts

Wooden spoon

Large glass serving bowl

Plastic wrap

Spoon

Serving bowls or glasses

¡FUERA! Go!

1. In a large heavy-bottomed saucepan, combine the water, rice, and salt. Bring to a simmer over medium heat. Reduce heat to low; cover with a lid; and cook until all the water is absorbed, about 12 minutes.

2. Use oven mitts to remove the lid. Use a wooden spoon to stir in the milk, sugar, and strips of orange zest. Increase the heat to medium and cook, stirring occasionally, until the mixture is thickened and creamy and has a porridge-like consistency, 15 to 17 minutes. Turn off the heat and slide the saucepan to a cool burner.

3. Stir in the vanilla. Pour the arroz con leche into a large glass serving bowl. Carefully cover the bowl with plastic wrap, pressing to make sure that the plastic is flush with the surface of the arroz con leche. Place the bowl in the refrigerator to chill for at least 8 hours or up to 3 days.

4. Spoon the chilled arroz con leche into serving bowls. Sprinkle individual portions with cinnamon and/or grated orange zest (if using). Serve.

 IT WAS EASY TO MAKE AND TASTED DELICIOUS."

—Colin, age 10

BRIGADEIROS
(CHOCOLATE FUDGE BALLS)

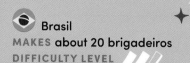 **Brasil**

MAKES **about 20 brigadeiros**

DIFFICULTY LEVEL

¡EN SUS MARCAS! Ready!

●●●○●●●●●●●○●●●

INGREDIENTS

1 tablespoon **unsalted butter**, plus more for greasing your hands

1 (14-ounce) can **sweetened condensed milk**

5 tablespoons (1 ounce) **Dutch-processed cocoa powder**, sifted (see page 21)

¼ teaspoon **kosher salt**

Vegetable oil spray

1 cup **sprinkles** (any color or shape)

¡LISTOS! Set!

●●●●○●●○●○●●●●●○●●●

EQUIPMENT

Rimmed baking sheet

Parchment paper

Large heavy-bottomed saucepan

Whisk

Rubber spatula

Small glass

Measuring spoons

Small bowl

Serving platter

Brigadeiros are small, fudgy, truffle-like candies from Brasil. They are usually decorated with sprinkles and served on tiny cupcake liners. I learned how to make them in middle school, in a class called "Actividades prácticas," or "Practical Activities." You just need to cook down sweetened condensed milk with cocoa powder and a bit of salt to get these rich and chocolaty candies. I'd call that a practical activity indeed! For this recipe I prefer to use Dutch-processed cocoa powder, but natural unsweetened cocoa powder will work, too.

1. Line a rimmed baking sheet with parchment paper. In a large heavy-bottomed saucepan, melt the butter over low heat. Add the condensed milk, cocoa, and salt and whisk until well combined. Cook until the cocoa is dissolved and the mixture is smooth, 3 to 5 minutes.

2. Increase the heat to medium and cook, stirring constantly with a rubber spatula, until the mixture starts to thicken and looks shiny, 5 to 7 minutes. It should pull away from the bottom of the saucepan when you drag the spatula across (ask a grown-up for help). Turn off the heat.

3. To test for doneness, fill a small glass with cold water. Scoop out ½ teaspoon of the chocolate mixture and place the measuring spoon with the chocolate mixture in the glass of water. Let it sit until the chocolate mixture is cool to the touch, about 30 seconds. Then squish it with your fingers—it should feel soft and fudgy. If it is not ready, return the saucepan to medium heat and cook for 1 more minute (just don't cook it for too long or the mixture will harden).

4. Spray the rubber spatula lightly with vegetable oil spray. Use the greased rubber spatula to scrape the chocolate from the saucepan onto the parchment-lined baking sheet and spread it out to cool (it won't reach the edges of the baking sheet). Let the chocolate mixture cool until it is cool enough to handle, 20 to 25 minutes.

5. Pour the sprinkles into a small bowl. Rub some extra butter on your hands. Portion and roll the chocolate mixture into 20 balls and coat them with sprinkles following the photos on the right.

6. Serve. (Brigadeiros can be stored in an airtight container at room temperature for up to 3 days or refrigerated for up to 1 week.)

CÓMO FORMAR LOS BRIGADEIROS
(HOW TO SHAPE BRIGADEIROS)

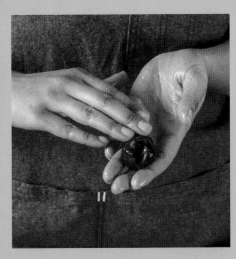

1. Scoop 1 tablespoon of the chocolate mixture and use your buttered hands to roll it into a ball.

2. Place the ball in the bowl of sprinkles and shake the bowl until the ball is covered all over. Transfer the brigadeiro to a serving platter. Repeat rolling with the remaining chocolate mixture—you should have about 20 brigadeiros.

ENSALADA DE FRUTAS
(FRUIT SALAD)

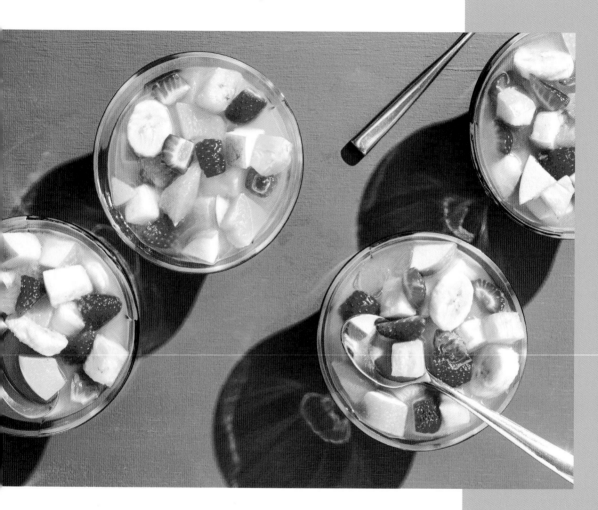

The ensalada de frutas I grew up with in Argentina is not your everyday fruit salad. Many different types of fruit are cut into bite-size pieces and soaked in citrus juice and ice cubes. In South America, Christmas falls right in the middle of summer, making a cold fruit salad the perfect holiday dish. The fancier the gathering, the more fruits I like to add to my ensalada de frutas. A basic version of this dish involves banana, green apple, pear, orange, and grapes. But to make it superfancy? Add pineapple. For me, pineapple smells like Christmas. That's when the pineapples are in season and affordable and taste amazing in Argentina. When I was growing up, my abuela always added a few spoonfuls of sugar to her ensalada de fruta.

🇦🇷 Argentina
SERVES 10 to 12 (Makes 12 cups)
DIFFICULTY LEVEL 🔪🔪🔪

¡EN SUS MARCAS! Ready!
●●•●●●●●●●●●●●●●●●●

INGREDIENTS

- ½ cup **lemon juice**, squeezed from 3 lemons (see page 20)
- 1 **green apple**
- 1 ripe **Anjou** or **Bartlett pear**
- 2 **bananas**
- 2 **oranges**, plus 2 cups **freshly squeezed orange juice**
- 2 cups (10 ounces) **strawberries**
- 1 cup ½-inch **pineapple** pieces (you can substitute canned pineapple in the winter)
- 1 (15-ounce) can **sliced peaches**, drained and chopped into ½ inch pieces
- 3 cups **ice cubes**
- 2 cups **water**
- 2 tablespoons **sugar** (optional)

¡LISTOS! Set!
●●●●●●●●●●●●●●●●●●●

EQUIPMENT

Large bowl

Cutting board

Chef's knife

Paring knife

Ruler

Rubber spatula

Serving spoon

Serving cups or bowls

¡FUERA! Go!
●●●•●●•●●●●●●●●●●●●●

1. Pour the lemon juice into a large bowl. Chop the apple, pear, bananas, oranges, and strawberries following the photos on pages 198–199, adding each fruit to the bowl of lemon juice as you chop. (This will ensure that the apples, pears, and bananas do not oxidize and turn brown!)

2. Use a rubber spatula to gently stir until the fruit is well coated with lemon juice. Add the pineapple and peaches to the bowl and toss gently to combine.

3. Add the orange juice, ice cubes, water, and sugar (if using). Gently stir to combine. Serve in cups or bowls with some juice spooned over top—the juicier the better! (The salad can be covered with plastic wrap and refrigerated for up to 3 hours.)

KEEP GOING

APPLES AND PEARS

1. Use a chef's knife to cut around the core to remove 4 large pieces.

2. Place the pieces flat side down on the cutting board. Slice each one ½ inch thick. Rotate the slices and cut crosswise (the short way) into ½-inch pieces.

ORANGES

1. Use a chef's knife to slice off the top and bottom of 2 oranges. Cut away the peel and pith (the white part) from each.

2. Cut each orange into quarters. Place the orange pieces flat side down, and slice crosswise (the short way) ½ inch thick.

BANANAS

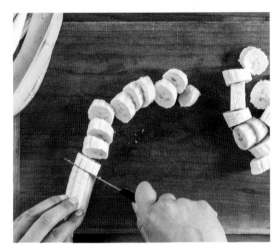

Peel the bananas and discard the peel. Use
a paring knife to slice the bananas crosswise
(the short way) ½ inch thick.

STRAWBERRIES

Use a paring knife to slice the strawberries in
half lengthwise through the stem end. Place
the strawberries flat side down. Use the tip
of the knife to cut out the green leafy parts.

PANQUEQUES CON DULCE DE LECHE

(CREPES WITH DULCE DE LECHE)

 Argentina

MAKES about 8 panqueques

DIFFICULTY LEVEL

¡EN SUS MARCAS! Ready!

INGREDIENTS

- 1 **large egg**
- ¾ cup **all-purpose flour**, sifted (see page 21)
- ¾ cup **whole milk**
- 2 tablespoons **unsalted butter**, cut into 8 pieces and softened
- 1–2 cups **dulce de leche**

  Confectioners' (powdered) sugar (optional)

¡LISTOS! Set!

EQUIPMENT

Medium bowl

Whisk

8-inch nonstick skillet

¼-cup dry measuring cup or 2-ounce ladle

Spatula

Plate

Small offset (icing) spatula

Serving platter

Spoon

Fine-mesh strainer

Panqueques are distant cousins of French crepes. The French version of a crepe is a thin, pale round disk often folded in fourths to serve, resembling a tiny handkerchief. The Argentinean version, which is my favorite, of course, is a little more forgiving. You can make your panqueques as thin or thick as you like, with a lot of browning. We roll ours up into tiny logs for serving. When I was a kid, my brother and I could never wait for my mom to finish making all the panqueques, so she would make the first one, cover it with dulce de leche, roll it, and cut it in half for the two of us to split. Against her advice, we would eat it with our hands, dulce de leche dripping down our arms. To this day, those were the best panqueques I have ever had.

1. In a medium bowl, whisk the egg until well combined. Add half of the flour and half of the milk. Whisk until well combined.

2. Add the remaining flour and milk and continue whisking until well combined and smooth. Let the batter sit for 5 minutes.

3. In an 8-inch nonstick skillet, melt 1 piece of the softened butter over medium-high heat. Pour ¼ cup of batter into the skillet and tilt the skillet slowly until the batter forms a thin, round layer and completely covers the bottom of the skillet (see the photo below). Cook until the bottom is golden brown, about 1 minute.

4. Use a spatula to carefully flip the panqueque. Cook until the second side is golden brown, about 1 minute.

5. Carefully slide the panqueque from the skillet onto a plate. Return the skillet to medium-high heat and repeat steps 3 and 4 with the remaining butter and batter, stacking the panqueques on top of each other on the plate. You should have 8 panqueques total. Turn off the heat.

6. Working with 1 panqueque at a time, use a small offset (icing) spatula to spread 2 tablespoons to ¼ cup of dulce de leche over the panqueque. Use your hands to roll the panqueque up into a log and place it on a serving platter. Repeat with the remaining panqueques and dulce de leche.

7. Add a spoonful of the confectioners' sugar (if using) to a fine-mesh strainer. Use the fine-mesh strainer to dust confectioners' sugar evenly over the panqueques, gently tapping the side of the strainer to release the sugar. Serve.

CÓMO HACER LOS PANQUEQUES (HOW TO MAKE THE CREPES)

Pour a ¼ cup of batter into the skillet and tilt the skillet slowly until the batter forms a thin, round layer and completely covers the bottom of the skillet.

¿QUÉ ES EL DULCE DE LECHE? (WHAT IS DULCE DE LECHE?)

Dulce de leche is a thick, sweet "milk jam" made out of cow's milk and sugar, cooked together for a long time. It's used all over Latin America, ranging in thickness and flavor. It's used for everything from a dollop on buttered toast in the morning to the filling in alfajores (page 188) to the gooey center of these panqueques. You can make it yourself or buy one of the many store-bought versions. Make sure to use a thicker dulce de leche for this recipe.

AGRADECIMIENTOS (ACKNOWLEDGMENTS)

I want to thank every single person at America's Test Kitchen Kids for making me look so good and helping give life to my dream; your dedication, professionalism, and talent show up in every single page of this book! You all are the best! But I need to add a superspecial THANK YOU to Molly Birnbaum, the editor in chief of America's Test Kitchen Kids, for having the wild idea to ask me if I ever wanted to write a children's cookbook—during a pandemic and remotely! Which gives me the opportunity to thank Adriana Stimola, my literary agent and friend, who held my hand and pulled me through this amazing and very nonconventional book-writing process.

Gracias to my brother Gonzalo Melian and my cousin Pablo Laurenzano, the other two cooks in the family, for helping me re-create Abuela Porota's magic. Obrigado to Armando Rafael for enduring some end-of-summer days in my very hot apartment kitchen to create the amazing cover of this book and make Pucho (my dog) and me look beautiful through your lens! To everyone who tested; tasted; read; helped me gather ingredients and wash dishes; listened to me rant about the book; and more, thank you! The list of names is long, and the order is random; this is the part where you think you will forget someone, but my friends are the best, and they will forgive me! So here it goes; gracias de todo corazón. I love you all . . .

Fede Poiana (por la paciencia), Ly Mateo (la mejor tía que Jersey City me dió), Allison Velez, Andrea Cataldo, Juliet Aguerre, Abigail Maldonado (y tus tías), Ana Saba, Devin Sanchez, Fanni Crespin, Rossana Salazar, Diana Cordoba, Edmundo Garzón, Ramona Rendon, Monica Escalada, Tina Perez, Aracely Rivera, Claudia Marino, Danisa Galop, Valeria Costa Buonocuore, Alicia Agosti, Laura Ahumada, Lester Suarez, Michael McLean (for introducing me to Luz), Nicole Raymond (que vivan las paltas), Stephanie Teekaram, Carla Marostegan, Valeria Aloe, Virginia Dimaio, Marina Recalde, Maria Virginia Portillo Decan, Zuleyma "Zuzu" Villa, Delia Balido, Susana Distefano, Diego Ruete, Lu Arjol, El Gordo Cocina (Victor Garcia), Leticia Amador, La Conga Supermarket, Central Valley Farm at the Van Vorst Park Farmers Market, and Jersey City. Thank you to all the artists and muralists who help make Jersey City so beautiful. And thank you to all the kids who came in to cook, eat, and participate in photos: Matteo, Eliot, Matilda, Nico, Georgia, Campbell, Teo, Zeniyah, Zoe, Maeve, and Lyona. And, of course, my mom—thank you forever and ever for teaching me that love is the most important ingredient in any recipe iy a seguir remando!

KEEP COOKING. BE HAPPY.

LOVE,
Gaby

CONVERSIONES Y EQUIVALENCIAS
(CONVERSIONS AND EQUIVALENTS)

The recipes in this book were developed using standard U.S. measures. The charts below offer equivalents for U.S. and metric measures. All conversions are approximate and have been rounded up or down to the nearest whole number.

VOLUME CONVERSIONS

U.S.	METRIC
1 teaspoon	5 milliliters
2 teaspoons	10 milliliters
1 tablespoon	15 milliliters
2 tablespoons	30 milliliters
¼ cup	59 milliliters
⅓ cup	79 milliliters
½ cup	118 milliliters
¾ cup	177 milliliters
1 cup	237 milliliters
2 cups (1 pint)	473 milliliters
4 cups (1 quart)	1 liter
4 quarts (1 gallon)	4 liters

WEIGHT CONVERSIONS

U.S.	METRIC
½ ounce	14 grams
¾ ounce	21 grams
1 ounce	28 grams
2 ounces	57 grams
3 ounces	85 grams
4 ounces	113 grams
5 ounces	142 grams
6 ounces	170 grams
8 ounces	227 grams
10 ounces	283 grams
12 ounces	340 grams
16 ounces (1 pound)	454 grams

OVEN TEMPERATURES

FAHRENHEIT	CELSIUS	GAS MARK
225°	105°	¼
250°	120°	½
275°	135°	1
300°	150°	2
325°	165°	3
350°	180°	4
375°	190°	5
400°	200°	6
425°	220°	7
450°	230°	8
475°	245°	9

CONVERTING TEMPERATURES FROM AN INSTANT-READ THERMOMETER

We include doneness temperatures in some recipes in this book. We recommend an instant-read thermometer for the job. To convert a temperature from Fahrenheit to Celsius, subtract 32 from the Fahrenheit reading, then divide the result by 1.8.

EXAMPLE
"Roast chicken until thighs register 175°F"

TO CONVERT
175 − 32 = 143
143 ÷ 1.8 = 79.44°C, rounded down to 79°C

ÍNDICE
(INDEX)